Jubilee, Sabbath, Sabbatical Year, ⟨ ⟩
laws are four pillars of God's governance—⟨ ⟩
shalom. Shalom is the overwhelming goodness of all relationships in creation. *Shalom* is ethical and it is necessarily economic. *Shalom* is about the ties that bind us—the policies, the laws, and the structures that order the way we live together in the world. As we sit in the shadow of a global pandemic that clarified the expendableness of "essential" workers and the protectedness of our ruling class, followers of Jesus are rightfully critiquing and interrogating traditional Western economic practices and values. In this context, Adam Gustine and José Humphreys offer *Ecosystems of Jubilee*, a profound and meticulous biblical framework for the divine economics of Jubilee. This book is a must-read. Then it is a must do.

LISA SHARON HARPER, president and founder of Freedom
Road, author of *The Very Good Gospel* and *Fortune*

José and Adam remind us that there has been an economic system in place that we have slipped away from and that inspires each of us to live out this just economy. *Ecosystems of Jubilee* is a must-read for anyone aspiring toward justice.

REV. DR. LEROY BARBER, executive director of Neighborhood
Economics, cofounder of the Voices Project

Most of us don't fully understand just how deep the mentality of scarcity is within us. Gratefully, there are shepherds like Adam and José whose words and lived experiences guide us toward gospel-informed neighborliness that can usher God's justice. In *Ecosystems of Jubilee*, we see how our spiritual practices are not separate from our financial decisions—and how, with intentionality, we can contribute to the liberation of others and ourselves through contemporary practices of gleaning, Sabbath, and Jubilee. The God of abundance draws closer through Adam and José's words. Will we choose to listen and act?

GENA RUOCCO THOMAS, author of *Separated
by the Border* and *A Smoldering Wick*

Our society's status quo bends toward scarcity, as José and Adam show so precisely in these pages. But their real contribution, the practical hope they offer to anyone ready to usher *shalom* into their neighborhood, lies in the beautiful vision for liberating abundance they find in Scripture. You'll find no spiritual platitudes or justice clichés here; the authors' wisdom has been gained over years of practical ministry in relationship with diverse communities. What you will find is a paradigm for local ecosystems in which everyone and everything can thrive. Read carefully, imagine creatively, implement collaboratively, and then keep your eyes open for the lasting fruits of righteousness and justice.

DAVID SWANSON, pastor of New Community Covenant
Church, CEO of New Community Outreach

This is the "better way" guide for community ethics we've been waiting for. Gustine and Humphreys take us out into the streets, where the abundant, generous, generative heart of God is vibrantly at work. Pastors and nonprofit leaders are sure to find this a fresh, imperative text. Even more, this blessedly practical book is for ordinary people who understand that "neighbor" is part of our spiritual DNA and simply need a nudge in the right direction. *Ecosystems of Jubilee* is a true place-changer. I cannot recommend it highly enough.

SHANNAN MARTIN, author of *Start with Hello*
and *The Ministry of Ordinary Places*

Gustine and Humphreys are serious about helping us all to understand what I call the Shalom-Sabbath-Jubilee Construct, and so was Jesus. If you don't understand Jesus's relationship to Jubilee, you have misunderstood him and his mission. *Ecosystems of Jubilee* faithfully leads us into a fuller understanding of this urgent topic and reveals how Jubilee can be implemented at various levels in our culture. Don't miss reading this book!

RANDY WOODLEY, PhD and author of *Shalom and the
Community of Creation: An Indigenous Vision*

If we want to see movements of restorative justice and joyful abundance in our lives and neighborhoods, we need a fresh imagination of economics rooted in the ancient story of God. Rev. Humphreys and Dr. Gustine have given us the theological and practical guide we need for this necessary journey. A book that is both timeless and timely. Highly recommended.

TIM SOERENS, cofounder of the Parish Collective,
author of *Everywhere You Look*

ECOSYSTEMS

OF

JUBILEE

ECOSYSTEMS

OF

JUBILEE

Economic Ethics for
the Neighborhood

Adam Gustine and José Humphreys III

ZONDERVAN
REFLECTIVE

ZONDERVAN REFLECTIVE

Ecosystems of Jubilee
Copyright © 2023 by Adam Gustine and José Humphreys

Requests for information should be addressed to:
Zondervan, *3900 Sparks Dr. SE, Grand Rapids, Michigan 49546*

Zondervan titles may be purchased in bulk for educational, business, fundraising, or sales promotional use. For information, please email SpecialMarkets@Zondervan.com.

ISBN 978-0-310-13355-1 (audio)

Library of Congress Cataloging-in-Publication Data

Names: Gustine, Adam L., 1982– author. | Humphreys, José, 1972– author.
Title: Ecosystems of Jubilee : economic ethics for the neighborhood / José Humphreys and Adam Gustine.
Description: Grand Rapids : Zondervan, 2023.
Identifiers: LCCN 2022052943 (print) | LCCN 2022052944 (ebook) | ISBN 9780310133537 (paperback) | ISBN 9780310133544 (ebook)
Subjects: LCSH: Social justice—Religious aspects—Christianity. | Christianity and justice. | Reparations for historical inustice. | Economics—Religious aspects—Christianity. | Theology, Practical. | BISAC: RELIGION / Christian Living / Social Issues | RELIGION / Christian Ministry / General
Classification: LCC BR115.J8 G87 2023 (print) | LCC BR115.J8 (ebook) | DDC 261.8—dc23/eng/20230110
LC record available at https://lccn.loc.gov/2022052943
LC ebook record available at https://lccn.loc.gov/2022052944

Cover design: Brian Bobel Design
Cover photos: © L. Feddes; Demerzel21 / Getty Images
Interior design: Sara Colley

Printed in the United States of America

23 24 25 26 27 28 29 30   /TRM/   12 11 10 9 8 7 6 5 4 3 2 1

*To my kids. Walking with you as you wrestle
out your growing convictions is an honor.
I hope this book helps all of us imagine new
possibilities to upend the old ways.*

—A. G.

*To the many churches reimagining new
agreements with money, labor, and land in
seeking a more liberating story for our world.*

—J. H.

CONTENTS

ACKNOWLEDGMENTS

In a book exploring issues of economic justice and the effects of economic exclusion, extraction, and exploitation on historically marginalized people groups, as well as on the land itself, we wanted to acknowledge our relative ignorance of the vast injustice that fills the timeline of the history of this nation. The stories and examples we share are but a small fraction of instances of oppression and victimization. There are multitudes of other people whose stories we don't know and whose names are lost to history. We acknowledge them, people who share the *imago Dei*, and lament the pain inflicted on, and justice unrealized for, them with little to no recourse.

Adam

I live in South Bend, Indiana, a city popularly known more for what it lacks than what it possesses. That is, in part, due to the story of this place as a microcosm of the forces of exclusion, extraction, and exploitation that we unpack in this text. It is true that we can tell the story of this city as the historic home of the Pokagon band of Potawatomi, a community I'm coming to appreciate as an exemplar in commitment to justice, reconciliation, and harmony despite their displacement and relative exclusion. We can tell the story as a series of shifts in demographics, though we would do well to note the way historic redlining and racially correlative economic divestment has fueled those changes. And we can tell the story as one often does in postindustrial midwestern towns, as a victim to economic forces beyond the control of those who bore the highest burden. When we tell the story of this town in those ways, we tell the truth. Truth that might open the door to justice. But we also miss the opportunity that has always existed in this city because the people who live, work, and play here represent the possibility of wholeness and restoration. There is so much good in the city because there are so many people. I'm thankful to live here and to be a part of this ecosystem. Not easy, but worth it.

Thanks, first of all, to José. It is always an honor to collaborate with creative, wise, and passionate people. Thank you for pushing this project to new depths and bringing your many gifts to bear throughout this process.

Thanks to Kyle Rohane and the team at Zondervan Reflective for the partnership and support throughout this project.

I'm honored to call a great many people coconspirators in trying to give expression to God's justice in the world. Some were brief partnerships; some are lifelong friends. All of them have left a mark on the thoughts and ideas shared in this book. On days when the challenges seem to overwhelm the possibilities, knowing that a great many others are waking up to resist the chaos of injustice in their communities is an encouragement to me to persevere.

Finally, thanks to Ann. I deeply admire your commitment to living a life of grace and justice. You bear the struggle of your calling with love and strength. Thank you for doing the local, ordinary, trying, and wonderful work set before you every day. I wish all people could have an example like you in their lives.

José

Most of my writing took place in East Harlem, the place I do ministry and call home. East Harlem is also the place of the original inhabitants, the Munsee Lenape peoples, on whose lands I am grateful to work. I also acknowledge the early labor of African Americans (enslaved and free) back when *Haarlem* was a Dutch village and the often-invisible labor of our immigrant community who make our city run today.

I want to thank Adam for the opportunity to collaborate on this project. Being able to partner with someone who is equal parts incisive and compassionate doesn't happen every day. I will hold precious the chemistry, rigor, and ease of our writing partnership.

I'm grateful for Kyle Rohane and the Zondervan team for seeing this vision forth and nurturing each step in the process with wisdom and grace.

There are lineages I carry into my work and practice, including the work of Dr. John Perkins and CCDA and the influences of Dr. C. Rene Padilla through his writings around *misión integral* (holistic mission). This work touched me personally through the mentorship of Dr. Raymond Rivera in the South Bronx. Also, the writings of Dr. Ched Myers at Barnabas Ministries challenged my imagination around economic theology.

My longtime friend Alexi Torres-Fleming at Jubilee Gift, Inc. is a voice the church needs to heed. A special thanks to Rabbi Hilly for pointing me back to the New Testament text in our early conversations about this project.

I'm grateful to my Metro Hope Church family, who continue to provide me with the laboratory for experiments in Jubilee. More recently, I've grown from my partnership with Jonathan Brooks, aka "Pastah J," and the Parish Collective fellowship. An invisible web tethers us across the boundaries of place and time.

To my life partner, Mayra. We symbiotically share a beautiful reality of what belonging and placemaking can be. And to my son, Javier: it is a joy watching you care for your friends; you've taught me how to love East Harlem again.

INTRODUCTION

What comes to mind when you hear the word *jubilee*? For most of us, it sounds like a celebration or the emotion of being overjoyed: jubilant! Some of us might think of celebrations we've seen or been part of or an anniversary of someone we admire: a couple, a pastor, even a queen. And, of course, you'd be right. Jubilee is a celebration, but it's much more than a party. Jubilee is a celebration with import. To declare *jubilee!* is to call for the world to take notice: *What is this cause for celebration?*

Scripture has much to say about jubilee. In the liturgical tradition of ancient Israel, Jubilee lasted a whole year. Every fifty years, the Year of Jubilee was a celebration with serious import; it was meant to reshape the very fabric of society. And that reason for celebration is the reason we wrote this book.

Our world gets bent out of whack in so many ways. Over time, and left to our own devices, the natural order of things drifts away from what we might refer to as God's intentions for humanity. After a while, we need some kind of God-ordained reset. (No, not a flood.) What we need is a mechanism to trigger a social restoration fostering renewed possibility for human and communal flourishing. That's why God gave Israel the Year of Jubilee. It was that social reset.[1] It was a communal restoration project. It was a way to put the pieces of a broken society back together again.

While we will talk about the particulars of the Year of Jubilee a bit later on, we want to start with this: Jubilee has the potential to help us reimagine justice. Jubilee was the pinnacle of a set of ethics, or practices, that God gave ancient Israel. Taken together with Sabbath laws and gleaning laws, the Year of Jubilee makes plain God's desire for justice to characterize the way the people of God organize their communities and the way they engage in the world.

Gleaning, Sabbath, and Jubilee were all cyclical. Gleaning laws dealt with the harvest season every year. Sabbath had weekly cycles as well as seven-year cycles. The Year of Jubilee occurred after every seven cycles of seven Sabbath years. In each case, we get a glimpse of the rhythm of God's justice that circles back toward healing, wholeness, and restoration. God created a cycle of justice to resist the natural slide toward injustice and inequity in the world.

All three of these—gleaning, Sabbath, and Jubilee—were also decidedly economic in nature. Certainly they dealt with many arenas of life, but at their core they aimed to recalibrate the economic status quo of ancient Israel. The economic ethics of the Old Testament were highly practical matters saturated by a theological vision that, if enacted, would set Israel apart as a particularly just society in the midst of a cruel, greedy, and unjust world—not unlike our world today.

So even though it's thousands of years old, the Year of Jubilee should be an accelerant to the moral imaginations of the people of God in our time. For those looking to enact God's vision for justice in the world, the Year of Jubilee helps create a framework that makes sense, even all these years later. The framework we will unpack will help us envision ways of building a more just world, starting in our own neighborhoods. We hope you've come to this book with a desire to envision and enact economic justice. And we hope this book is a helpful part of that work.

Learning the Hard Way

I (Adam) have been thinking for some time about my first foray into engaging with the economic questions of justice and the church. I was taken by the idea that developing a creative economic initiative could open up possibilities for individual and community transformation that the traditional church or nonprofit structure simply couldn't manage. I didn't just hope it could work; I knew it could. I'd just moved to northern Indiana from New York City, and I had seen firsthand the ways innovative economic projects could act as a "front of house" for significant community development or justice work in the neighborhood. I also knew that these kinds of creative combinations fired up the imaginations of those who wanted to "do good" in ways that mere volunteerism never seemed to do and certainly couldn't sustain over the long haul. I was leading a small band of idealistic folks eager to make a difference in ways that demonstrated a God-oriented concern for whole people and whole communities, and we wanted to see what was possible.

The result was a pie shop.[2] But our vision was for something much more. We found an incredible space in the middle of a neighborhood that, while not experiencing extreme poverty exactly, was certainly hardscrabble and often overlooked by the wider community. We had a strategy for creating pathways to greater economic vitality for individuals experiencing significant challenges. The general idea was for a short-term work development opportunity providing transitional income and job training to help people in crisis situations find long-term work.

As I reflect on this short-lived (some of the reasons for that I outline below) project, I think we had more than just our hearts in the right place. We were doing a few things I'd commend even now. First, we were trying to take the economic part of our humanity seriously. Economic vulnerability is almost cancer-like in the way it corrupts the capacity for individuals and communities to thrive. As you'll see throughout this book, we believe that the root causes of injustice and oppression are almost always connected to—if not driven by—economic concerns. So any attempt at working toward justice and the good of a community that fails to consider economic questions is not thinking seriously enough about the problem and does not see God's full intention for cosmic restoration. This is an idea we will tease out throughout the book, but specifically in chapter 1.

Second, integrating economic questions into our community development initiative forced us to humanize the work. Looking back at it now, this was a project that aimed to advocate for folks whom others might be inclined to disregard and demean. We were attempting to create a community where dignity was seen and celebrated as opposed to the status quo of society where economically vulnerable folks live at the margins of wealthy society and interact with the rich in oftentimes demeaning ways—as recipients of depersonalized service or charity, in on-the-street interactions, through low-wage labor in culturally denigrated forms of work, and more. I think our work was trying to challenge that, and even though I didn't have a full appreciation for it at the time, it celebrated human dignity and the dignity of work in ways that are essential to the pursuit of economic justice.

Third, our model developed around an emerging food scene that catered to upwardly mobile folks and those with more discretionary income than most. This strategy had flaws, but there was something embedded in this approach that is helpful to highlight as a key feature of economic justice in local communities: because neighborhoods do not exist in isolation from one another—even if they are segregated and/or sequestered from one another—the economic realities in one community are influenced by the economic realities in another, and vice versa. (In chapter 2, José will unpack this idea by comparing neighborhoods to ecosystems.)

We intuited that the impact of our project, and not just the financial bottom line, depended on being a bridge between the resource-rich areas of our city and the resource-lacking areas. We were betting that the resource-rich foodie scene could afford to come to the community and buy expensive pie, and in turn pie could act as a conduit for capital to flow back toward more economically vulnerable folks. We weren't thinking about it this way at the time, but it seems to me that the idea was to leverage the pie shop in a kind of "business as Robin Hood" way, where the shop worked to redistribute money from the wealthy toward those experiencing poverty.

But despite those positives, this project failed to gain much traction. And I've spent the intervening years trying to puzzle out just why that was. Beyond circumstantial reasons (of which there were many), there were a few things we didn't take seriously enough as we prepared and launched this project.

Perhaps most significantly, we failed to grapple seriously enough with the magnitude of the economic barriers that existed between us and the folks we hoped to help. Back then I found myself saying, "Make it as human as possible," and I think we did a decent job with that. Our pilot work development program was highly intentional, and the folks who helped run it were extremely thoughtful. We thought we understood the challenge of creating community among a group of folks with such disparate economic realities in daily life. But in the midst of the work, we were exposed to the depth of our blind spots. For one, I was learning on the fly the kind of economic pressures faced by folks on public assistance and the enormous chasm that had to be crossed to get from public aid to economic self-sufficiency. These folks wanted to become self-sufficient, but countless obstacles in their paths made it nearly impossible. These obstacles jeopardize a person's ability to find or maintain economic stability if that person isn't set up for financial success from the start. These new friends were proof positive that the Americanized "bootstraps" model of economic progress was a lie. The folks we were working with dealt with things I had never experienced for myself. We might have resided in the same city, but we were living in two different worlds. As Martin Luther King Jr. might say, we were living in two different Americas.

Two Americas

In the year before his death, King gave a speech called "The Other America." His words were delivered with a timbre of solemnity, as if he were giving a eulogy for the myth of a singular American experience. Instead of a vision of America as a land of plenty and opportunity for all, Dr. King laid plain the reality of injustice and economic inequality.

> There are literally two Americas. One America is flowing with the milk of prosperity and the honey of equality. That America is the habitat of millions of people who have food and material necessities for their bodies, culture and education for their minds, freedom and human dignity for their spirits. That America is made up of millions of young people who grow up in the sunlight of opportunity.[3]

This picture dominates the narratives of our nation's history that suppose this experience is normal for most US citizens. King surely invoked the imagery of Israel's journey to the promised land overflowing with "milk and honey" with intention. Accustomed as many American Christians are to incorporating religious imagery into our civic discourse, particularly those images that paint the United States as a kind of second Israel—chosen by God as a beacon to the world—King's confrontation of the unholy marriage between Christianity and American society was a direct challenge to people of faith in the United States. He continued,

> But as we assemble here tonight, I'm sure that each of us is painfully aware of the fact that there is another America, and that other America has a daily ugliness about it that constantly transforms the buoyancy of hope into the fatigue of despair. . . . By the millions, people in the other America find themselves perishing on a lonely island of poverty in the midst of a vast ocean of material prosperity.[4]

King was describing a vast swath of American society. People cut out and excluded from the "milk and honey" prosperity promised by the American dream. He was describing communities destroyed by urban planners who disregarded the dignity of families rooted in neighborhoods in cities across the country. He was describing the obvious and eventual outcomes of economic policies that favored the already wealthy over the poor, white over Black, and citizen over immigrant. He was describing generations of folks who grew up without feeling the "sunlight of opportunity" shine on them, those rays blocked by the monuments of privilege and relative aristocracy built by the residents of the first America.

So, America has never been one America. As King highlighted, the first America is known for its prosperity and opportunity. It is characterized by ample resources for flourishing life that provide onramps to joyful exploration of the world's gifts. The second America is the opposite kind of community. On the surface, it is challenged by lack of work, decreased economic flourishing, and threats to life and well-being with barriers that impede the pursuit of the wider joys of the world. It corrupts natural human hopes into despair.

King drew a line between the two Americas, in a sense rejecting the notion of a middle class of folks who reside between the rich and poor. King seemed to be suggesting that, *middle class* or not, there is no *middle ground* when it comes to economic justice. In some ways, the middle class probably experiences economic injustice alongside the poor. In other ways, the middle class probably perpetuates and even perpetrates economic injustice alongside the rich. That puts middle-class folks in a position of responding to the challenges of justice with some sense of personal experience and responsibility. So, for those of us who might consider ourselves middle/upper-middle class (as we would), we encourage reading this book through the lens of being residents of King's first America, because we might be uniquely positioned to be a conduit for justice in these matters.

These two Americas are divided, but they are also related. They did not arise in separate spaces, unimpacted by each other. They are intertwined. The story of this nation is, tragically, a story of the interrelated experiences of the haves and have-nots, of oppressed and oppressor, of dominated and dominator. As we will see throughout this book, the material prosperity of the first America was established, and is maintained, on the systemic and interpersonal degradation of those who live in the other America. This economic injustice often goes unseen, is conveniently overlooked, or is hypocritically denied by residents of the first America.

This was the dynamic working behind the scenes of the pie shop. We didn't appreciate the extent of the interrelated nature of our existence. We wanted to connect the neighborhood/neighbors we were working with to the upwardly mobile, resource-rich people outside the community, but we didn't have a deep enough understanding of how the systems that benefit some work to the detriment of others, supposing instead that we could simply act within that system and produce transformational good. We needed to do more work to think through how our economic project might disrupt a system that supports a divide between the two Americas, or how we might nurture an actual alternative to the system that excluded and marginalized these folks to begin with. We were responsible to do more than offer a job development program. That leads to a second reason this project was shortsighted.

My Responsibility for My Neighbor's Welfare

Economic disparities are rarely, if ever, value neutral. They are the natural outworking of injustice, systemic inequality, racism, and classism—concrete manifestations of sin and the brokenness of humanity. The divide between the two Americas is unnatural and unjust. God does not desire economic divides that lock people into degrading forms of poverty while securing more wealth for others.

In our experience, this economic divide is one of the barriers standing in the way of economic justice, even at local levels. Because our current economic system is so fragmented and depersonalized, our economic choices feel pretty inconsequential. Our daily buying, spending, trading, and selling definitely don't feel like a way of supporting vast systems of inequity. But not understanding the interconnected nature of our lives in community is one of the main reasons why we have such a hard time—particularly in the church—of grappling with systemic expressions of injustice. It is easier to blame "the poor" for poverty than to question systems, cultures, and practices that create conditions for economic hardship to thrive, in particular, if we are doing well ourselves. Many people cannot point to a single instance where they personally exploited the poor, which is good. But when lined up against centuries of economic injustice perpetrated against Black, indigenous, immigrant, and low-income populations, we should be humble enough to question whether we are unintentionally complicit in the evil of economic injustice.

But there is a different way to think about this. Iris Marion Young, in *Responsibility for Justice*,[5] contrasts the ideas of guilt and responsibility. She contends that there is a difference between being guilty of injustice and being responsible for injustice or, more specifically, responsible for correcting injustice. She proposes what she calls a "social connection model"[6]—a model strikingly similar to the theological notion of the *common good*—and argues that we are not absolved of responsibility for justice even if we have not specifically committed an act that can be directly connected to an injustice. This is because we participate in and benefit from a system that produces injustice. This participation, even when unintentional, and benefit, even when tangential, create a sense of corporate responsibility. Because we live in a society where injustice exists, the nature of our human interconnectedness creates a kind of moral responsibility for each of us to work to make things right.

One of the reasons Young's notion is so compelling is that this is where discussions around justice often break down, particularly among Christians. Despite the fact that our faith tradition acknowledges a sense of fundamental guiltiness—think original sin—sometimes we struggle to apply this logic to the way our society functions. But Young changes the conversation. She shifts the discourse away from determining the degree of guilt we bear for past injustices by calling our attention to essential human connectedness and suggesting each of us is individually responsible to participate in the work of justice.

Take, for example, the conversation around reparations for slavery and racial injustice throughout the history of the United States (a topic Young addresses as well). This conversation often breaks down because it feels offensive to be considered guilty for things someone never "personally" did. But trying to prove guilt in this sense is not always the most fruitful exercise. (Note: We would never advocate for *ignoring* the question of guilt for historic and modern-day economic oppression. These are serious and sober discernments that deserve to be worked out today and, to the extent those enacting oppression can be identified, to deal with it.) Instead, looking to the future requires a framing that invites participation by everyone rooted in a different kind of moral logic. If we are bound together socially, such that our collective well-being is tied up in one another, then we are responsible to attend to the circumstances and conditions that prevent folks from thriving. Young's model helps us find ways forward on these traditionally tricky conversations.

Duke L. Kwon and Gregory Thompson's book on reparations frames the work of reparations as a "call to repentance and repair."[7] This is a compelling way of framing not just the question of reparations but all matters of economic injustice. Repentance is a matter of identifying ways that are out of alignment with God's intentions and that produce the fruit of sin or injustice. Repentance also includes a willingness to act differently, a turning from old ways and toward new ways. This is a decidedly Christian way of admitting that we are responsible for the way things are and the way things should be. Kwon and Thompson suggest that a Christian view, in regard to questions of reparations, calls us to consider practices of restitution, restoration, and repair. We find ourselves in agreement and want to commend their excellent contribution to the way we think of economic justice practices generally.

Repentance, restitution, restoration, repair—this set of *R* terms reminds us of John Perkins's famous set of three *R*s for the work of Christian community development: relocation, reconciliation, and redistribution.[8] We find Kwon and Thompson's set of *R*s a helpful way of extending and nuancing Perkins's ideas.

For economic justice to take root in a community, it begins first with a work of repentance on the part of the rich—not only a recognition of their position of social advantage over the poor but also an honest work of confession related to the tangible injustices inflicted on the poor by their choices and lifestyle (intentional or not). This repentance must go beyond admission of wrong and result in a turning away from current economic practices toward those that yield justice. As people of faith, this includes acknowledging ways the church has acted as "perpetrator . . . accomplice . . . silent bystander,"[9] and to then recognize that "this history implicates us all."[10] To be implicated in historic injustice is, à la Young, not necessarily an accusation of guilt, in the forensic sense, but it is to say that we are included as participants in its modern effects, and we are key players in the possibility of change for the good.

Second, economic justice must include straightforward restitution for the poor. We need look no further than the story of Jesus's interaction with Zacchaeus (Luke 19:1–10) to see how a recognition of economic injustice demands that those who profit from injustice make things right in concrete ways. Zacchaeus's interaction with Jesus reveals that he has dealt dishonestly and unjustly with the powerless in the community by cheating them financially through overtaxation. His act of repentance was to give back, over and above his offense, to any and all he had cheated. It is true that Zacchaeus was responsible for his specific actions, and his restitution was related directly to that. However, the unjust actions he was perpetrating were accepted as the status quo at the time. After all, "the ancient tax collection system promoted nothing less than 'institutionalized robbery,' and Zacchaeus was one of its best robbers."[11] That makes Zacchaeus's actions a confrontation of injustice rather than only an individualized response. His act of repentance was an active accusation of a larger system, and we miss this layer if we think of this only in individualized terms. Zacchaeus was a standard-bearer in the case for seeing reparations as part of the work of responding to the reality of participation in a system of economic injustice. He did not conveniently ignore the economic debt he—as a member of the wealthy class—incurred toward those he and others oppressed through unjust means. Instead, he sought to make restitution a tangible response of his repentance.

Third, economic justice requires that we pay attention to the breakdown of society's DNA caused by oppression, and that we creatively and tangibly work to promote restoration and repair. Kwon and Thompson highlight the relational nature of restoration, a reweaving of the fabric of society damaged by injustice. In their view, the parable of the good Samaritan outlines the way in which restoration is the outworking of Christian love.[12] In addition to restoration is the call to repair. If restoration is the outworking of love to repair the social fabric of society, we see the call to repair as the invitation to restructure the systems of society and mend the collateral damage injustice has done in tangible ways in community. The prophet Isaiah envisioned as much, noting after a long call for relational expressions of God's justice that when justice is done, the people will be known as "Repairer[s] of Broken Walls, Restorer[s] of Streets with Dwellings" (Isa. 58:12). Later, in the chapters on Sabbath, we will return to this notion of restoration and think about it in more comprehensive ways.

When I consider these many layers in relation to our pie shop, we didn't take our responsibility for our neighbor's welfare seriously enough. As a result, it made the work we were doing in the neighborhood more superficial than we intended. We weren't grappling with all the deeper issues, and we didn't really wrestle with our participation in broken systems and our responsibility to act differently in the world. It was certainly an exciting new venture, but one prone to overlook ways we could have done some deeper work, both internally and in the community.

For example, although we tried to celebrate the dignity and value of each person we engaged, we needed to do more than just see dignity, because recognizing dignity connects us to larger issues of justice. Dr. King was an exemplar in weaving together the notions of inherent dignity and its connection to economic justice. On March 18, 1968 (less than one month before he was assassinated), he visited Memphis, Tennessee, to speak to a gathered crowd concerning the unjust treatment of sanitation workers in the city. In his speech "All Labor Has Dignity," he said, "So often we overlook the work and the significance of those who are not in professional jobs, of those who are not in the so-called big jobs. But let me say to you tonight, that whenever you are engaged in work that serves humanity and is for the building of humanity, it has dignity, and it has worth."[13]

The recognition of human dignity is itself a call to seek justice. Notice how King made this connection. He told Jesus's parable of the rich man and Lazarus from Luke 16, in which a rich man ignores the plight of poor Lazarus and, in so doing, seals his eternal fate. Dr. King said the rich man

> went to hell because he didn't see the poor. . . . There was a man . . . in need of the basic necessities of life, and [the rich man] didn't do anything about it. . . . There's nothing in the parable that says [he] went to hell because he was rich. Jesus never made a universal indictment against all wealth. . . . [The rich man] went to hell because he allowed Lazarus to become invisible . . . because he allowed the means by which he lived to outdistance the ends for which he lived . . . because he sought to be a conscientious objector in the war against poverty.[14]

Citizens of the first America cannot be conscientious objectors in this work because we are active players in a divided world that exacts punishment on the poor. To disengage from the work is to perpetuate injustice. Jesus left no doubt about the priorities of God and the expectations of God toward those with means. While I'm not sure our pie project made us conscientious objectors, we certainly weren't as proactive in opposing injustice as we might have been. Targeting the upwardly mobile's discretionary dessert-based income was never going to move the needle for the community, without some deeper interventions alongside. Had we been more proactive, we might have thought through ways of mitigating some of the bigger issues that stunted any potential impact we might have had with this work—starting with the question of who owned the project to begin with.

Ownership and the Year of Jubilee

As our title suggests, we see the Year of Jubilee as the lynchpin of economic justice, a vision for a way of life that keeps the wheel on the axle of society. The Year of Jubilee is not only a way of making things right for a society bent out of whack, but it is also an enactment (for an entire year!) of the society God envisions.

This is important for us to consider because the essence of Jubilee helps shape a moral framework for the people of God today. Not only is this because the Old Testament is rife with examples like this where writers explicitly articulated

God's intentions as they described what a just and good society looks like but also because we believe Jesus said so as well. In Luke 4 Jesus framed his ministry as declaring the "year of the Lord's favor" (Luke 4:19, quoting Isa. 61:2), which is at least an oblique reference to the Year of Jubilee, if not a full and direct connection to it. By doing this, Jesus was declaring an unending Year of Jubilee inaugurated by his ministry. Jubilee is central to the eschatological promises of God's liberation. As we will see, this liberation is cosmically inclusive, yet it prioritizes the poor. Jesus said as much in Luke 4, where he coupled the declaration of God's Jubilee favor with the proclamation of "good news to the poor" (v. 18). Luke 4 frames Jesus's vision of his ministry. The economic ethics of the Old Testament are not diminished in Christ; rather, they take on enhanced meaning in our collective imaginations. A thoughtful and concrete vision for Jubilee can animate our hope and our action toward God's intentions in the present day.

One of the primary problems that the Year of Jubilee was meant to correct dealt with the question of ownership. We will take a deeper dive throughout this book, but for now, the Year of Jubilee was a reset button on who owns what. During Jubilee—meant to occur every fiftieth year—land was returned to its familial roots. If your family had lost their land, it was to be returned. Also, during Jubilee, debts were forgiven and slaves were released. In each of these cases, we see the crucial role ownership played in fostering a just society. Who owns the land? Who owns the capital? Who owns the people themselves? Central to Jubilee is liberation and ownership over the things (land, capital, self) that create the conditions for economic vitality.

Our fledgling pie shop project didn't take questions of ownership and the prioritization of the poor into account. At the end of the day, the project was still part of a larger nonprofit, which meant the economic possibilities of taking ownership were seriously stunted. There is still so much good that can be accomplished through the traditional nonprofit means, but the notion of Jubilee opens up the possibility for more. Without considering ownership, we will struggle to do more than offer services to others.

I've tried for the last several years to ask harder questions of myself and others about who owns what. My experience working on these questions in on-the-ground and denominational roles gave rise to many interesting possibilities and experiments that attempt to take the question of ownership seriously. This is a conversation we return to in later chapters.

The Structure and Shape of the Book

So much of our shared disposition is that theology, and working for justice on-the-ground, is like jazz: contextual, improvisational, personal, and interpersonal. The stories we share aren't meant to be applied wholesale to every context; they are meant to inspire you to improvise and contextualize them in your particular setting within your specific community.

This is also how we come to the text of Scripture. We recognize that there are many ways to come to the text and myriad methodologies that shape theological reflection. Throughout this book, we are attempting to read the text in ways similar to how we hope you utilize this book. As we read the accounts of the people of Israel and encounter the vision laid out by various writers, we want to allow that ethical framework for a good and just society to animate our imagination for what that might mean for us today. Certainly, theological reflection is predisposed to making connections and teasing out implications for topics outside the bounds of "theology" narrowly defined. Our work is an attempt to imagine a world as guided by these scriptural ideals.

Taken at face value, the ethics outlined in the scriptural texts we will explore together are God's intentions for God's people. They are directives that not only demonstrate a concern for being faithful to God's intended ways but also produce a society more capable of promoting human and communal flourishing. If the people of Israel were hearing these laws as explicit commands of God, then taking them seriously today might create ways of experiencing something of the good and beautiful world God has in mind for all of us.

In part 1 of this book, we explore some foundational elements of our shared vision for economics and justice—namely, that bondage is universal, that the gospel is about liberation, and that the freedom offered in the gospel extends to concrete economic realities of life. In short, rich and poor alike need the freedom of the kingdom of God. We then explore the nature of neighborhood life and contend that neighborhoods are interconnected and interdependent ecosystems that rise and fall as one. It is in that context of an interconnected life in community that we work out the ethical framework we unpack in this project. How can we extend the gospel of God's liberation to tangible day-to-day life in the neighborhood?

In part 2, we examine the core notions of this book,

unpacking the Old Testament economic laws related to gleaning, Sabbath, and Jubilee. These three form a kind of triad of economic ethics. Taken together, they help us picture the kind of society God had in mind and explore the economic inflections of those intentions. While we explore each in their biblical contexts, we will also situate their ethics in our present social and cultural moment. What do these Old Testament notions say to us today regarding economic justice?

Finally, in part 3 we imagine what it might mean to embody the values and practices of this economic ethical framework in our world for individuals and communities concerned with economic justice and flourishing at the neighborhood level. Jesus came declaring the year of the Lord's favor. What does it mean for us to live into that proclamation now?

The experience of trying, and failing, to create an expression of economic justice has stuck with me (Adam) for many years now. We had a few things right and got a few things wrong. But that experience has served to deepen my passion and sharpen my convictions about the essential elements of economic justice initiatives in local neighborhood spaces. And thankfully, I know I'm not alone. Many folks who live in the first America have tried and are trying to cultivate expressions of economic justice in their communities as well.

Because of that, we don't write this book as a total excoriation of the first America. Instead, we write to widen the population of folks—Christians in particular—who are not only concerned about poverty and economic injustice but are also bringing their best and most creative thinking to the conversation around how we might address these issues.

Both of us have lived and worked in each of Dr. King's

Americas. The content of this book is deeply personal because we bear witness to the realities of economic injustice every day. We aren't claiming to have it all figured out, but we want to help extend the conversation toward action in pursuit of an economic community God envisions in the world.

With that in mind, this book is unapologetically theological. The gospel demands that Christians pay attention to injustice and work toward expressions of economic justice in the world. In writing from an explicitly Christian perspective, we hope this book is something of a celebration of the wide and long love of Christ that extends into the specific realities of our brokenness and begins to redeem us, even now, through the power of the Spirit at work in and through the people of God in concrete places. At the same time, this book is a reminder that God has an overwhelming concern for the poor and vulnerable populations of people on the economic margins of our society. The scriptural narrative leaves no room to doubt the passionate way God "resides" alongside the poor—many times in direct opposition to the rich—and demands justice on their behalf. This fact is often ignored, glossed over, or explained away. Our full attention is required not only to see that God *prefers* the poor, but then also to ask hard questions about what that means for all of us in daily life and practice.

So while Christians are not the only players in the work of economic justice, people of faith should be at the forefront of dismantling the divide between the rich and poor. This work is simultaneously personal and corporate, internal and external, local and broad. It is massive and complex. But we don't throw up our hands at the complexity. Instead, we engage with the community right in front of us, recognizing that we cannot do everything but can do something. Collectively, we can care for the communities into which we have been placed and begin the work of justice in our own backyards. From there, we trust that God will give each of us vision for our participation in larger work and broader engagement.

But we must start now. We cannot miss the urgency of economic justice. If you are interested in engaging, learning, and starting to work out the priorities of God, economically speaking, we hope you find this book a helpful companion on the journey.

PART ONE

JUBILEE, LIBERATION, AND THE NEIGHBORHOOD ECOSYSTEM

In part 1, we consider some of the aims of this book and frame the telos of the work of nurturing God's economic vision in local communities. Jubilee is a celebration of liberation: slaves set free, debts released, land returned. These fundamental elements of the Year of Jubilee as outlined in Scripture represent tangible, economic liberation. Liberation, though, is not meant merely for the oppressed, but for the oppressor as well. We are all in bondage to the captivity of wealth in different ways. Jubilee is freedom, and we will explore what that means.

We also frame the bulk of this project in the context of local neighborhoods and communities. We write about ways the gospel and God's justice can take root in local spaces with neighbors we know on the sidewalks we walk together.

Though spatially limited, neighborhoods are richly complex and not always easy to understand. At the same time, we realize that not everyone lives in a community where folks across the economic spectrum intersect in natural ways. As you begin to think about the interconnectedness of communities (and in an increasingly globalized world, an argument could be made that we are always more interconnected than we even realize), we encourage you to consider how you might begin to engage this work in your context. It is highly unlikely that there is a community where each member of the community is thriving economically. Begin to envision what it might look like in your community for each person to thrive.

Conceiving of neighborhoods as ecosystems and training ourselves to think ecosystemically—learning the natural ways in which neighborhoods create and sustain human flourishing—are essential characteristics of those who can effect change and foster God's shalom in their communities.

ONE

JUBILEE IS FREEDOM

What does it mean to be free? Our answer to that question is critical for this entire conversation. That's because the biblical notion of Jubilee is ultimately about liberation—the freeing of land, freeing of capital, freeing of people themselves. One of the central ideas of this book is that liberation and economic justice go hand in hand. If we want to nurture healthy ecosystems of God's Jubilee, we need to take questions of oppression and liberation seriously, and we need to consider the economic layers of that oppression and envision the economic fruit of that liberation.

If liberation and economic justice go hand in hand, it stands to reason that the opposite is also true. And when oppression and economic injustice pair up, it usually looks like exclusion, extraction, and exploitation. In other words, economic injustice will almost assuredly express itself as one of those three things—people being left out of the economic life of society, people being robbed of their economic potential, people being used for others' economic gain. One could make the argument that the economic system of the United States is built on a commitment to exclusion, extraction, and exploitation.

Slavery is a paradigmatic example of economic injustice in US history. An economic system that depended on the economic exclusion of an entire segment of society, while simultaneously exploiting enslaved people to extract profit from their labor, is a fundamental cause of the wealth and prosperity of this nation. Of course, there are countless other examples, large and small, of ways the injustices of exclusion, extraction, and exploitation manifest themselves throughout our shared history. They show up in people's direct actions, but they are also embedded in the systems and customs of our society. Civil rights attorney Brian Stevenson is famous for saying that slavery didn't end, it just evolved. Of course, he is right, because even though slavery was abolished, constitutional amendments did not deal with the unjust DNA of exclusion, extraction, and exploitation. Because those things are still active in our economic life, economic injustice continues to flourish.[1]

The work of economic justice then, requires pushing back against the forces of exclusion, extraction, and exploitation, and creating new systems to resist the slide toward injustice over time. Because those three *E*s create systems of oppression, economic justice is fundamentally a question of freedom. To say that we want to work for economic justice is to say that we want to work for the liberation of those who are excluded from, extracted from, and exploited by a society organized to produce those outcomes.

In Scripture, the Year of Jubilee means freedom. Jubilee frees up capital, land, and the people themselves. It was meant to have concrete effect in society.[2] But Jubilee is also a theological notion designed to shape our imaginations for a different way of being together in the world.[3] That way of being together is possible through the undoing of oppression and in the cultivation of communities that reflect God's intentions—even God's economic intentions—for our life together.

Liberty or Liberation?

I (Adam) grew up, like many of us, saying the Pledge of Allegiance every day in school. Hand over heart, without really knowing what I was doing, I swore fealty to a set of American[4] ideals, each day finishing with the commendable aspiration of living in a nation with "liberty and justice for all." I was raised to believe freedom was inextricably connected to being an American. Now, we all know that American ideals are aspirational. That is, we are all, collectively, trying to reach a vision we suppose the founding fathers had for us. But as I grew up and learned quite a bit more history, it seemed to me that these ideals weren't aspirational as much as they just ignored reality. I pledged allegiance to a flag that was understood to represent liberty and justice for all, and yet we know that wasn't always the case. As a kid, I didn't fully understand what was happening, but as an adult I recognize that saying the pledge day in and day out was helping me ignore or overlook reality in favor of an American ideal of freedom. Liberty and justice for all is a noble ideal, to be sure. But in our society, it's also a myth that leads us down all manner of unhelpful paths.

In the United States, being free is often articulated as the total autonomy of individuals, whereby people are at liberty to determine for themselves everything about their lives through any matrix of decision-making they wish. For many of us, even the possibility of constraint is agitating. Pandemic mask ordinances enflaming tensions around freedom and individual liberty is one example of this at work. Ordinary people throwing off the shackles of N95-esque tyranny fit with this ingrained myth of American liberty. Many people took great pride in emulating that rhetoric and couching it as patriotism.

So we might say that liberty, or the right to life without constraint, is an American value. But it is a hypocritical one. One of the great myths of this nation's history is its supposed dedication to liberty, when a mere cursory reading of our history demonstrates that the wealthy and powerful have always enriched themselves and their communities and solidified their "life without constraint" by constraining the freedom of others. The liberty myth has thrived in the American consciousness for so long, many cannot recognize its dangerous duplicity.

Even more troubling, the myth of American liberty has co-opted the imagination of many streams of the church in this nation. The history of Christianity in the United States contains a tragic through line of syncretism. In other words, we have a long history (in some church traditions) of combining American values with Christian values and conflating freedom in Christ with American liberty.

Maybe you've seen this like I have. I've been in churches that had a (not surprising) tug-of-war over the presence of the American flag in the sanctuary, making the flag seem like a holy relic. I've been in churches that sing patriotic songs as hymns around US holidays. I've seen a verse like John 15:13 ("Greater love has no one than this: to lay down one's life for one's friends") divorced from its connection to Jesus and applied to military personnel. This is not an argument against patriotism as much as it is a red flag for the ways religious practice uncritically intertwines with national identity and values. Anytime we find gospel/theological metaphors doing heavy lifting for American ideals, we have discovered syncretism at work.

This was certainly in the water of the church world I grew up in. And it had a huge influence on the kind of Christian I was trying to be. For me, being a "Christian" meant I was deeply invested in a particular set of political outcomes, as if the future of God's kingdom depended on it. And I know I'm not alone. For much of our history, it was possible to believe that certain segments of the American church had been caught up in a wave of spiritual fervor that left us a bit naive and open to being co-opted by political powers. In recent years, it has become clear that it was not naivete at all, but an intentional move on the part of politicians and leaders of the church in America, largely within the Protestant evangelical movement, to solidify a power base that would shore up their rights to autonomy at the expense of others. Scholars of religion in the United States have thoroughly chronicled the history and development of this reality in the overall evangelical movement and the Christian church at large.[5] Often this power was solidified at the expense of vulnerable populations. Marginalized and socially excluded groups have paid the price for the unholy alliance between church and state in US history.

One of the ways this syncretism proliferated was through overspiritualization of the notion of freedom. It's possible to interpret Romans 8:2, where we read that Christ has "set you free from the law of sin and death," as the writer, Paul, suggesting that other issues of oppression are not in the purview of the gospel's liberation. This line of thinking would give slave owners and antebellum preachers permission to "preach Christ" to enslaved peoples and still demand they stay in bondage. Salvation, liberation, justice—these are spiritual realities, not tangible ones. The divide between spiritual and tangible realities has stuck in many churches such that, over time, we've perhaps gotten used to a Jesus who saves us from our sins and leaves the rest of it alone. This represents a reduction or distortion of the gospel.

This is the same gospel distortion identified by Howard Thurman when he wrote, "It cannot be denied that too often the weight of the Christian movement has been on the side of the strong and the powerful and against the weak and oppressed—this, despite the gospel."[6] Carl F. H. Henry said, in his 1947 book, *The Uneasy Conscience of Modern Fundamentalism*, that what became the evangelical movement was largely and "perpetually indifferent to the problems of social justice."[7] Instead of holding together what we might call the "spiritual" and "concrete" realities of the gospel, those realities were separated, and in many cases the "spiritual" realities of freedom in Christ were wedded to abstract notions of national identity in the United States. Embracing an overspiritualized gospel helps injustice continue to thrive. It also distances us from the gospel Jesus set in motion.

The Gospel as Liberation

In our society, liberty is often framed as a static notion or a state of being. I either have liberty or I do not, and many in our society are trained to react to real or perceived infringement upon that liberty. That's one reason why conversations about liberty and freedom often devolve into selfish or self-centered arguments about what's mine or what I'm free to do.

But the gospel gives us a better way to think about what it means to be free. We contend that instead of this shallow and selfish notion of freedom trotted about in so many circles, the gospel is not about so-called liberty, but liberation. The gospel as liberation actually *frees* us from the self-centered notions of liberty.

Dietrich Bonhoeffer, martyred anti-Nazi dissident and founding member of the Confessing Church during World War II, helps us distance ourselves from possessive, self-centered notions of freedom by reminding us that the gospel's conception of freedom means that we are set free *for a particular purpose.* "Freedom is not a quality of man . . . because freedom is . . . not a possession . . . but a relationship and nothing else. In truth, freedom is a relationship between two persons. Being free means 'being free for the other,' because the other has bound me to him. Only in relationship with the other am I free."[8] We will explore the way freedom creates a sense of solidarity and mutuality later on, but for now note the way the experience of freedom is neither static nor selfish. The American myth of liberty confuses us in both regards.

Liberation, on the other hand, is active. Liberation suggests that one lives in a state of captivity and in need of freedom. Liberation is the process of being set free from captivity. It tacitly acknowledges that a whole host of things may hold a person captive and encourages the pursuit of a more thorough-going liberation.

To say that the gospel is not about liberty but liberation is an intentional choice on our part. We do not believe the gospel lives in the binary. It does not deal with static states of being. Rather, the gospel is the good news of God continuously liberating people from various captivities. Even more, to believe the gospel is to believe that everything is always being set free in Christ. This is what Paul was arguing in Romans 8. Rather than an argument for a spiritualized version of freedom, Paul, in this critical text, was making the cosmic argument for the gospel as liberation. Paul wrote, "Creation itself will be liberated from its bondage to decay and brought into the freedom and glory of the children of God" (v. 21).

In the midst of a stirring articulation of the glory of the gospel and the resurrection realities that accompany it, Paul paused and turned his attention from the personal to the universal. The bondage to sin and death experienced by each person is mirrored by the bondage to death and decay experienced by all of creation. This is no toss-away line. It is central to Paul's argument that while the people of God are experiencing something unique related to Christ, it is not an exclusive experience. The entirety of creation is locked up in captivity to its own decay, and the good news of Jesus contains the promise of a universal liberation. The gospel is not only a matter for spiritual cardiologists; it is good news for the entire cosmos.

Liberation—Always, Ongoing

This liberation is being enacted by God through Christ, but Paul indicated that it is something we have yet to fully experience. Liberation is a process, and that process nurtures a longing for more liberation. Because in Christ everything is always being set free, it also must be said that everything is always experiencing the pain of its own captivity. Paul acknowledged as much in Romans 8: "We know that the whole creation has been groaning as in the pains of childbirth right up to the present time. Not only so, but we ourselves, who have the firstfruits of the Spirit, groan inwardly as we wait eagerly for our adoption to sonship, the redemption of our bodies" (vv. 22–23).

Notice here the essential mutuality between "the whole creation" and the "we" of the church. Rather than divide out and separate the church from the rest of the world based on supposed spiritual realities, Paul chose to focus on our essential commonality with the rest of God's creation. As the gospel makes us aware of our captivity and deepens our longing for liberation, it draws us into a greater experience of solidarity with the rest of creation.

Solidarity is at odds with one of the main flaws of the myth of American liberty—that is, the way it encourages viewing others as a threat. We might view immigrants with suspicion, supposing they are coming to take something that belongs only to us. We might look down on those who require public assistance because they "take our hard-earned tax dollars." We might distrust "governmental overreach" because policies constrict self-determination at some level. Perhaps it is because we are a nation founded on violent rejection of perceived oppression, but our default mode seems to assume that our liberty is under threat. That's not a posture that sets the stage for good conversation about justice.

The gospel, however, invites us into the conversation from a different place and with a different posture. The gospel liberates us to discover our *shared* experience of bondage. We are all locked up in what Paul called "bondage to decay," meaning that we experience pain, brokenness, relational breakdowns, societal inequity, global violence and chaos—the list could go on. Paul said we should not be surprised by all that. Creation itself is groaning in pain, as are those who have the firstfruits of the Spirit in them. Paul wanted us to see that being in bondage to decay is common to all creation, humanity included. No part of creation remains exempt from this captivity. There's no separation, just a shared need to be set free. We all carry wounds of death, disease, and disharmony. We are bruised by the brokenness of the world, and we find all manner of ways to bruise one another—even those we know and love deeply. We cannot walk through the world and escape the experience of feeling captive to the effects of sin and death. Being sealed with the firstfruits of the Spirit is not an automatic exemption. Rather, the Spirit gives us a language to articulate our longing for liberation. Even if, as Paul said later in Romans 8, the Spirit's language isn't always intelligible to those of us who call out with it; it is the voice we speak with in the world.

This is the starting point for understanding the gospel as liberation. The gospel of liberation is rooted in captivity and suffering. The gospel animates the imagination of people who know they are in bondage, helping them channel their suffering toward the hope that everything is always being set free in Christ. It challenges those who pretend to exist in a state of liberty and exposes ways in which that "liberty" actually encourages oppression by those who deny or don't see their own captivities.

Remembering Bonhoeffer, out of a shared need for liberation comes the shared experience of freedom, which can only be fully received in relationship with others. When Christ sets us free from our captivities, he frees us into a cosmic community where we experience and work out this freedom together.

A "Preference" for the Poor

It is important to highlight here that even though captivity is common to all creation, *it is not experienced the same way by everyone.* One of the dangers of an overspiritualized gospel is the way it erases the particularity of people's experiences. It is essential for us, rather than letting the shared experience of bondage to mute the distinctive ways people experience it, to allow that common experience to sharpen our ability to see the specific ways in which bondage works. In other words, rather than saying, "You're in bondage, and so am I. Therefore, I know exactly what you're going through," we ought to say, "You're in bondage, and so am I. Therefore, I should be heavily invested in learning more about the specifics of your bondage." This is an essential point of the principle of the "preferential option for the poor and vulnerable." Championed by liberation theologians among others, the preferential option for the poor and vulnerable rests on the acknowledgment that the experience of the oppressed or marginalized is unique. Yes, everyone is in bondage, but those who experience captivity based on their membership in a particular social subgroup experience a double portion of oppression's negative effects.

For example, the rates of overincarceration of Black and Latino men and women is as literal a form of captivity as imaginable. Despite the lack of data supporting a heightened degree of inherent criminality in those communities, the scourge of mass incarceration manifests itself in the continued decay of communities and evidences how our collective need for liberation takes a higher toll on more vulnerable populations.[9]

Similarly, race is an independent predictor of whether a person lives in a community with dangerous levels of environmental hazards. Studies show that 60 percent of people who live within zones deemed environmentally unsafe are Black or Latino.[10] It would, of course, be naive to think that such racialized disparity is coincidental. Instead, this is a reality brought about by neglect and the intentional targeting of communities of color. Not only have generations of these communities grown up exposed to toxic waste in their neighborhoods, but zoning measures and public perception hurt possibilities for selling properties or relocating to safer communities, consequently locking people up in hazardous communities for the foreseeable future.

Human history is full of examples of how poor and vulnerable people groups are marginalized, exploited, and victimized by the structures and values of dominant societal groups around them. The biblical story itself is the story of such a people. Israel is oppressed by its dominant neighbors throughout the Old Testament, and the historical context of the New Testament is one of a subjugated people wrestling with ideas of liberation and freedom while under the thumb of an oppressive power.

These biblical accounts are significant because they demonstrate that huge swaths of the recorded work of God are of God announcing and enacting liberation in the context of captivity. High points in the biblical narrative include the story of Israel's bondage in Egypt and God's liberative work in the exodus. So, too, do we find allusions to liberation in the story of Jesus, as the New Testament writers were keen to draw parallels between the work of Christ and the imagery of Israel's liberation. The promise of being set free from bondage is an undeniable theme throughout the entire narrative of Scripture.

The promise of liberation nurtures an eschatological hope within the community of captivity. This was one of the primary functions of the Old Testament prophets who came to the people during times of physical captivity to lift up the eyes of the people to see a future where God liberates them and restores their fortunes. Eschatological hope animated the people's way of life, calling them to act now in light of a future reality. Considering again Paul's words from Romans 8:22–23, note that he described creation's groaning, not like a dying man, but like a woman in childbirth who, despite the severity of her pain, can sustain herself in the knowledge that the pain she bears is a "firstfruit" of new life. This is not a "redemptive" suffering in which a good end justifies the experience of suffering. Rather, eschatological hope is a response to the revelation that redemption locates itself within suffering. The people are not abandoned to their suffering for God is present within it, enacting liberation.

The fact that God is present to the people in their suffering challenges attempts to frame "future hope" as a call to passive acceptance of current circumstances. Instead, the promise of liberation functions to critique the status quo of captivity. The prophets of the Old Testament consistently pair the revelation of God's liberative intent with an exposure of injustice and the oppression it enacts. Set against the promises of God's liberation, the prophets carefully and particularly name the experience of captivity as something happening to God's people and, at the same time, something being done by God's people. The call for justice *now* is not just a salve for the people who are oppressed by "outsiders," it is also an as-needed condemnation of the people's way of life together.

Consider Micah's famous charge "to act justly and to love mercy and to walk humbly with your God" (Mic. 6:8). This command follows the beautiful vision of God's liberation in action where Micah said,

> Come, let us go up to the mountain of the LORD,
>   to the temple of the God of Jacob. . . .
> He will judge between many peoples
>   and will settle disputes for strong nations far
>   and wide.
> They will beat their swords into plowshares
>   and their spears into pruning hooks.
> Nation will not take up sword against nation,
>   nor will they train for war anymore.

Everyone will sit under their own vine
　　and under their own fig tree,
and no one will make them afraid,
　　for the LORD Almighty has spoken. (4:2–4)

Similarly, God's rhetorical questioning of the people in Isaiah 58:6 ("Is not this the kind of fasting I have chosen: to loose the chains of injustice and untie the cords of the yoke, to set the oppressed free and break every yoke?") is bound up with the promise of liberation and justice:

Then you will call, and the LORD will answer;
　　you will cry for help, and he will say:
　　　　Here am I.

If you do away with the yoke of oppression,
　　with the pointing finger and malicious talk,
and if you spend yourselves in behalf of the
　　　　hungry
　　and satisfy the needs of the oppressed,
then your light will rise in the darkness,
　　and your night will become like the noonday.
The LORD will guide you always;
　　he will satisfy your needs in a sun-scorched
　　　　land
　　and will strengthen your frame.
You will be like a well-watered garden,
　　like a spring whose waters never fail.
Your people will rebuild the ancient ruins

and will raise up the age-old foundations;
you will be called Repairer of Broken Walls,
Restorer of Streets with Dwellings. (58:9–12)

The eschatological vision of God's liberation is the tie between the gospel and justice. Because the gospel reveals that everything is always being set free in Christ, we have good reason to question ways of doing theology that normalize or overlook the tangible experience of oppression and bondage. We also have serious cause to champion theological and practical work that seeks to nurture liberation as a revelation and application of the gospel at work in the world. The preferential option for the poor seeks to locate the gospel primarily where Paul located it in Romans 8: in the experience of captivity.

If the gospel is not proclaiming liberation for captives, it is not the gospel of Jesus. Howard Thurman picked up on this notion in *Jesus and the Disinherited*, saying, "I can count on the fingers of one hand the number of times that I have heard a sermon on the meaning of religion, of Christianity, to the man who stands with his back against the wall. It is urgent that my meaning be crystal clear. The masses of men live with their backs constantly against the wall. They are the poor, the disinherited, the dispossessed. What does our religion say to them?"[11]

In addition to calling us to recognize the importance of a gospel that roots itself in the experience of the oppressed, Thurman also exposed the missteps of the proclamation of the gospel in America and highlighted the divorce between the spiritual and concrete experience of oppression at work in society and the church. This is the great gift of liberation theology as well. Like the Old Testament narrative and prophetic tradition, liberation theology provides an eschatological vision for the gospel's liberative work in a way that prophetically challenges the status quo of modern-day oppression.

Catholic priest Gustavo Gutierrez notes that liberation provides three "interpenetrating layers of meaning" that are instructive for us. Theologically, we see liberation at work in Christ, who "liberates man from sin, which is the ultimate root of all disruption of friendship and of all injustice and oppression. Christ makes man truly free."[12] This is what we've been arguing all along: that the scriptural testimony proclaims a gospel where everything always is being set free in Christ.

Historically, though, Gutierrez calls us to see liberation as a kind of responsibility, a mutual indebtedness to the reality of the human story in which "true freedom leads to the creation of a new man and a qualitatively different society."[13] This means that the liberation of Christ has a social effect. It ought to impact and influence the character of our societies in a way that reform and social change are expected.

Gutierrez argues that liberation also nurtures the longing for liberation among those under the thumb of oppression. It "expresses the aspirations of oppressed peoples and social classes . . . at odds with wealthy nations and oppressive classes."[14] This is in line with Paul's notion that all of captive creation is "groaning" or longing for liberation and supports the idea that the prophetic vocation (both in Scripture and the work of the people of God) is to nurture an eschatological hope for liberation. Taken together, it is easy to see why Gutierrez seeks to frame the gospel around tangible liberation in the context of the violence and oppression of Central and South American dictatorships.

This understanding of liberation is also why James Cone could draw powerful parallels between the crucifixion of Christ and the horrific history of the lynching of Black people in America.[15] He located the redemptive possibilities of the cross in the experience of suffering, not to justify it, but to acknowledge the lived experience of oppression and to declare God present to the people *in their suffering* and enacting liberation from that space. These prophetic streams, both in the Black and liberation theology traditions, have found imaginative space in the story of God's bondage-breaking work for Israel to proclaim a vision of the good news that is authentically welcome among communities of those whose backs are against the wall.

More personally, liberation is expressed in the vision of the God who inhabits the suffering of oppression and captivity with the possibility of redemption that motivated the personalism and charity of Dorothy Day.[16] Her generosity and compassion, no less radical than the theological work of Gutierrez and Cone, led her to position herself in the midst of the suffering of others, recognizing her inherent need for liberation and thus her solidarity with those on the margins as well. Seeing Christ in the face of the poor was a hallmark of her way of life and the way of life she inspired in so many others.

The Liberative Gospel in an Economic Landscape

Taking our cues from Romans 8, there is a certain universality to economic bondage. In other words, it goes both ways:

economically speaking, both the rich and the poor need economic liberation, though the exact nature of their captivity is unique.

For the rich, the reality of their wealth reinforces the walls of their prison. Jesus highlighted this in Luke 12 when he told the story of a "certain rich man" who stored up his treasures. Jesus said his very life would be "demanded from" him (Luke 12:20). He spent so much time in the pursuit of increased wealth that he found himself constructing the bigger barns of his own enslavement. Jesus indicated that all this "worry" entraps those who pursue unchecked wealth and "we incur a debt to the future that we cannot repay."[17] Later on in Luke 18, Jesus interacted with a rich young ruler, asking him to divest of his wealth in order to prioritize the plight of the poor, and the man walked away sad because his wealth had created a prison from which he could not free himself.

We see this enslavement to wealth in many ways today. Families saddle themselves with enormous mortgages to satisfy their "bigger barn" impulses. They take on overwhelming debt in the pursuit of leisure and chase the mirage of "opportunity" for their kids in sports, music, and academics—presuming their wealth has provided a gateway to security. This captivity to wealth creates such a strong sense of entitlement that people commit crimes in the name of securing a future for themselves and their families, as evidenced by the shocking college admissions scandal of 2019.[18]

One of the great tragedies of the captivity of the wealthy is the way enslavement masquerades as freedom. Too often we live under the illusion that wealth makes us free, when in reality we are in a prison of our own making. In John 8:31–36, we find that Jesus illustrated the ease with which we mistake our enslavements for freedom.

> To the Jews who had believed him, Jesus said, "If you hold to my teaching, you are really my disciples. Then you will know the truth, and the truth will set you free."
>
> They answered him, "We are Abraham's descendants and have never been slaves of anyone. How can you say that we shall be set free?"
>
> Jesus replied, "Very truly I tell you, everyone who sins is a slave to sin. Now a slave has no permanent place in the family, but a son belongs to it forever. So if the Son sets you free, you will be free indeed."

Here we see that Jesus's famous proclamation of the freedom he came to offer was said in response to a community of people who confused privilege for freedom. Their perceived priority of place lulled them into believing they had no need of liberation. It is not hard to see the same thinking surrounding the way many seek to obtain and maintain wealth. Jesus came to set the rich free from their bondage to their own wealth.

However, while the rich are indeed *captive* to wealth, they are not the recipients of *injustice*. Historically, they are the *perpetrators*. It is a matter of deep lament to recognize that the wealthy often demonstrate their captivity through the oppression of the poor—through exclusion, extraction, and exploitation. This is a story that stretches back, again, to the Old Testament, when God took issue with the economic oppression of the poor by the rich, saying, in Isaiah 58:3, "Yet on the day of your fasting, you do as you please and exploit all your workers."

In the same way, the oppression of the poor by the rich is condemned in New Testament texts like James 5:1–5, where the writer says,

> Now listen, you rich people, weep and wail because of the misery that is coming on you. Your wealth has rotted, and moths have eaten your clothes. Your gold and silver are corroded. Their corrosion will testify against you and eat your flesh like fire. You have hoarded wealth in the last days. Look! *The wages you failed to pay the workers who mowed your fields are crying out against you. The cries of the harvesters have reached the ears of the Lord Almighty.* You have lived on earth in luxury and self-indulgence. You have fattened yourselves in the day of slaughter. (emphasis added)

Today the economic oppression of the poor continues in the form of predatory lending, delinquent landlords, the bail/bond system, unlivable wages, unsafe working conditions, and detrimental governmental policies that create barriers for the poor in their pursuit, not of wealth, but of basic human sufficiency and flourishing. These are but a few of the myriad ways in which the wealthy and powerful enact deeper injustices and do so in a way that widens the economic gap between the rich and poor.

But it does not have to be this way. One of the aims of this book is to demonstrate different expressions of our common captivity, while nuancing the specific injustices that the rich—and the society created to work for them—exact on the poor, which exacerbate the experience of oppression faced by marginalized communities. Being truthful about the particular way economic oppression works itself out in the world can create a space from which we then narrate a vision for a movement of redemptive possibility. Our hope is that we all might come away from each chapter with a stronger grasp of the reality of economic injustice and an appreciation for the opportunity that exists to see people set free.

In other words, the gospel that is setting everything free, all the time, has good news for those whose backs are against the wall *and* for those whose fingers are bruising the breastbones of those backed into the corner.

Scripture outlines a pathway toward the practice of economic justice at the personal and local level. The urgency and importance of an engaged people of God seeking to enact God's vision of Jubilee in our communities cannot be overstated. Returning to Romans 8, we find that Paul began this section related to the captivity of all creation with this stunning line: "For the creation waits in eager expectation for the children of God to be revealed" (v. 19).

All of creation is waiting, yes, for liberation from God, but also all of creation is waiting—in eager expectation!—for the children of God to be revealed. Hopefully it's not a stretch to suggest that this line could read, "All of creation is waiting with bated breath for the children of God to show up!"

Why?

Because the creation that groans—like a mother in childbirth—knows that the people of God are the midwives of liberation. We may not bring liberation into being—that is God's work in Christ. But our theological frame allows us to see the moral imperative to work for liberation in society and to hear the cries of the oppressed as they long for liberation. We align ourselves alongside the captives and accompany all of creation in a shared journey through suffering, pointing to and enacting evidence of God's liberation along the way.

This is the work we are called to as people of faith. It's a calling we forget sometimes. Rev. Raymond Rivera, founder of the Latino Pastoral Action Center, says, "Too often, we fail to understand God's plan for our lives, or we simply reject his call to be instruments of liberation and restoration for the people, institutions, and systems and structures in our society."[19] We have been set free *for the other*. As people of faith, we walk through the world with two choruses echoing in our heads and hearts. We hear the voice of Jesus singing, "If the Son has set you free, you will be free indeed," in harmony with one of the great prophets of the civil rights movement—Fannie Lou Hamer—reminding us that "nobody's free until everybody's free."[20]

TWO

NEIGHBORHOODS AS ECOSYSTEMS

I (José) am a plant dad—or so I've been called. I nurture about forty plants that are strewn throughout our apartment in East Harlem. The majority are nestled in a corner room with windows facing both south and east, which provide the soft light of sunrise and the more intense light of the afternoon. When I began collecting plants, I began with a snake plant, or what we call at home, "a hard to kill plant." These starter plants were important for my plant journey, especially since for some time a green thumb seemed elusive. After some moderate success in growing, nurturing, and even repotting this plant, my inner voice of discernment said, "The snake plant is looking pretty lonely these days." Not to be deterred, I began adding other plants, like small succulents, which could withstand direct sunlight and drier conditions. Following these were ferns, which preferred more shade and more humid conditions. Upon some further intense research via Google, I even learned that placing plants in proximity to each other could serve as a natural humidifier. This meant I could organize my little plant huddle in ways that each plant could benefit from the presence and proximity of the others. Before I knew it, I was tending to my own neighborhood of plants within the concrete jungles of East Harlem.

Knowing that within our apartment space, plants are working together with us to create healthier conditions, to receive the sun from our southeast-facing windows, to convert sunlight into food and oxygen, feels very connectional to me. We get to foster our own micro system of well-being. Also, witnessing the harmony and well-being sustained by elements like soil, water, and light also piqued my interest in how plant life works together in the larger world of nature.

I learned from a documentary called *Intelligent Trees* how trees networked in a forest can actually communicate with one another. Through their research, scientists uncovered how subterranean root systems can foster communication between trees, alerting them to danger and need. The roots of these trees can also serve as channels for the exchange of resources that promote the well-being of individual trees. A malnourished tree in a highly shaded area can send distress signals to neighboring trees. As a result, it will receive carbon and other minerals from surrounding trees, even when trees are located at a significant distance from one another. The exchange of nutrients is made possible through an underground root system. This "wood wide web" in some ways parallels our own virtual World Wide Web. Communication, multiple transactions, connections, and exchanges occur below the surface of the soil, making the story above the surface harmonious and fruitful.

Nature merely confirms the elegance and harmony of God's ecosystem, what the ancient Hebrews referred to as *shalom*—when things are in right relationship with one another. At its best, shalom reveals God's creation operating in a harmonious relationship so that creation can flourish. These nourishing transactions and exchanges form a cosmic kinship, a relationship between people, places, and things. Ultimately, God's operating plan for creation is to be cultivated and sustained through the human community.

If nature says something about the qualities of the Creator (Rom. 1:20), nature can also provide the church with the wisdom to become humbly situated and in right relationship within a neighborhood ecosystem. Much like forests, neighborhoods in cities, towns, or rural areas are interdependent, spatial realities, made up of systems and interrelated conditions. Hence, God's invitation to faithful presence as a church is rich in complexity and teeming with possibility.

Neighborhoods as Ecosystems

Take a few moments and close your eyes. Begin to imagine what a healthy, flourishing neighborhood looks like. What does the architecture communicate? What kind of space might sidewalks provide for social engagement? How do neighbors typically engage with one another? What does the range of class diversity (or lack thereof) say about this place? What role does the church play in daily common life, if any? How are different institutions functioning to serve the common good? What does individual well-being look like as you stroll the streets?

A meditative exploration can train our awareness into ecosystems thinking, to see ourselves as part of a larger whole in a neighborhood. Our participation in the daily life of our local worlds can be guided with the Holy Spirit's wisdom. With sacred curiosity, we can begin to contemplate the right conditions needed to sustain healthy life in a neighborhood. For followers of Christ, this is a form of contemplative inquiry that goes beyond a neighborhood assessment. Rather, it is a way of looking at a neighborhood with God's imagination and intent for physical places. Willie Jennings writes, "A Christian doctrine of creation is first a doctrine of place and people, of divine love and divine touch, of human presence and embrace, and of divine and human interaction . . . Christianity is in need of place to be fully Christian."[1]

When we think of place, we can think of water sources, educational institutions, public parks, sewage systems, adequate housing, local government; houses of worship that provide spiritual care; museums that preserve history and culture, and small businesses for the exchange and purchase of goods and services. These are just some of the systems that make up a neighborhood ecosystem. Another way of viewing this is through the view of "the commons," the resources that people share that cover areas such as: education, culture, economics, and civic engagement.

When we trace Jennings's theological thinking here, neighborhoods can be considered deeply spiritual, spatial realities. Essentially, they can be signs and echoes of what is "very good" about God's creation. Neighborhoods can mirror the deep spiritual realities of the good creation when it fosters individual and communal flourishing. Conversely, neighborhoods can also become ghettos for the rich, the middle class, or those impacted by poverty, where groups live segregated.

Our historical reality demonstrates that neighborhoods can mirror what poet Langston Hughes described as "A Dream Deferred." For all our civilizational advancements, deep disparities still remain around who gets access to adequate resources for human thriving. Even today, what we often consider thriving neighborhoods can be more often than not enclaves for the privileged, where people can seal themselves off from those impacted by poverty and its affects. The system has set up neighborhoods to act as isolated units lacking the mutuality needed for flourishing. One might ask, "What contributes to these conditions?" Some of the answers can be traced back to how Americans have imagined place over history.

Stunted Memories and Social Vulnerabilities

Neighborhoods, whether located in cities, towns, or rural areas, have been imagined by planners, politicians, and local boards. Typical neighborhoods like mine have community boards that work together with local government to determine budgets and how resources are allocated. Having participated in some of these boards, I know there are many well-meaning people who have common interests in mind. But often the historical memory of the neighborhood does not factor into assessing its current conditions. But often lost in the deliberations around neighborhood well-being are the historical insights connected to present inequities. Lost are factors such as segregation, mass incarceration, and even the historical impact of redlining. Yet the echoes of historical injustices still impact many neighborhood ecosystems today.

To put this in context, it is well-documented how redlining practices created geographic barriers that favored white neighborhoods throughout the country, redirecting Black buyers to less-desirable neighborhoods. Redlining was a corrupted form of mutuality through exclusivity, where Realtors, neighborhood planners, and the government all colluded to keep neighborhoods white. This strategy used a map that color coded neighborhoods, labeling them on a range between desirable and undesirable when selling property to white people. Redlining was also a determinant of which bodies were worthy of living in specific places.

Consequently, redlining not only created segregated neighborhoods, but it was the exercise of white sovereignty over space, where neighborhoods became emanations of white supremacy. To this day, redlining has left a legacy of "social vulnerabilities" connected to negative health outcomes, incarceration rates, and educational attainment in neighborhoods throughout the country, with New York as a prime example.[2]

Legacies of redlining can be seen in places like New York, which has one of the most segregated school systems in the country. Enormous disparities exist in New York connected to race and class, determining which children will have access to a quality education. Since public schools are partially funded on a neighborhood's tax base, the lower the tax base, the less resources the school will have. Ultimately this represents a disordered relationship between different systems within the ecosystem, namely, economics and education. Think of these two systems as root systems that are vital for the personal and economic well-being of a neighborhood.

To illustrate this further, take a school in Scarsdale, a suburb in Westchester, New York. This is a school that is typically well resourced; students have a classroom environment (think ecosystem) where the conditions are ideal for learning. A single teacher might have twelve children in a classroom, and they have access to the latest technology. Community capital is represented here through professional parents who can cultivate generative connections with other parents in the parent-teacher association (PTA). The PTA relies on these parents to make healthy donations whenever the school identifies needs not covered by its own budget.

Conversely, inner-city schools receive fewer funds and often suffer from overcrowded classes with limited resources. I recall my wife working for a vibrant, beautiful, yet poverty-impacted after-school program in Washington Heights. She once described how one class met in a tractor trailer to accommodate a large overflow of students. Students faced all kinds of challenges from the lack of resources; the setting in which these children had to learn was overly stimulated, with teachers spending most of their time managing child behavior.

Right Relationship Is Everything

For those who wonder if lower educational attainment is a reflection of the morals and work ethic of these communities, the research proves differently. When students, regardless of race, are given the same educational opportunities under the same conditions, all can thrive at the same levels. Even more striking is when Black teachers teach Black students, the achievement levels can be positively impacted. Research shows that Black gifted and talented students are more readily identified by Black teachers. In contrast, a study shows that "regarding teacher expectations . . . when evaluating the same black student[s], white teachers expected significantly less academic success than black teachers."[3]

In another study, social scientists recently combed through the records of a hundred thousand Black students in North Carolina throughout the duration of five years. What they found was that having one Black teacher between the third and fifth grade reduced the chance that an African American boy would later drop out of high school by 39 percent.[4]

On an individual level, a Black teacher might bring to the classroom (in addition to skill and competency) the visceral experience of knowing what it is to be overlooked, hence tailoring their teaching to meet their students' needs. Additionally, they will also be more well acquainted with the larger forces at work, attuned in more nuanced ways to the needs of Black children.

Without serious consideration for right relationship in addressing educational disparities in schools, society will continue to relegate Black and brown children to being intellectually inferior. These stunting conditions in the neighborhood ecosystem feed other related conditions—for example, a school-to-prison pipeline. Where underperforming, overcrowded schools are ill equipped to deal with Black and brown children, the culture of the school often defaults to reinforcing punishment for misbehavior. This culture of classroom policing and supervision becomes a natural onramp that leads some to a life in and out of prison.

What if the church, on a micro level, took on the same mindfulness of the Black teachers mentioned previously? As we focus on larger systems, we cannot overlook how micro-level interventions can feed larger systems the intel needed for structural improvement. What difference can followers of Christ make in their localized efforts to seek shalom? This is one of the ways the church can begin to wisely discern injustices on a multiplicity of levels, in ways that are rooted in right relationship to people and places.

Rightly Rooted

Gustavo Gutierrez once described sin as "a breach of friendship with God and others [and] . . . according to the Bible the ultimate cause of poverty, injustice and the oppression in which persons live."[5] These relational breakdowns persist when people do not see themselves as friends, or even potential friends, bound together within an ecosystem. With this lack of sight, there is a lack of awareness or empathy for those within our radius who suffer from the impact of poverty and systemic injustices.

In contrast, righteousness or right relationship, according to Scripture, is to be in alignment with what matters most to God. And to know what matters most to God is to know Jesus and his priorities. This is the intimacy of friendship. Jesus told his disciples in John 15:15, "I no longer call you servants, because a servant does not know his master's business. Instead, I have called you friends." Similarly, in Matthew 25:31–46, when Jesus tells a story about the great judgment, he relates it through the ministry of vicariousness. Those who fed the poor, gave water to the thirsty, and visited the prisoner actually *knew* Jesus, because to serve the least of these meant to serve him. Vicariousness then goes deeper than simply saying we represent Christ. Vicarious acts of justice come from intimate connection to God and others. Our good works in this world make their way to heaven and are done as unto Jesus!

Cooperation and collaboration are channels through which the church can nourish the neighborhood, on earth as it is in heaven. One might notice that each of the people Jesus mentions: strangers, those who experienced homelessness, hunger, and disabilities, all represent parts of our neighborhood ecosystems today. Yet the nature of the call is to receive and host Jesus again and again in our connections and mutuality with "the least of these."

Inherent in each encounter is something that the privileged can learn from societies' most vulnerable. Dr. Michael Mata, urban missiologist, calls this dynamic exchange a "mutual transformation," where space is made for those on the receiving end of support to become teachers with Jesus for the benefit of those with privilege. These learning moments enlist the privileged to Christ's priorities and practices among the most vulnerable.

Real friendship is cultivated through the intimacy that comes through mutuality. Biblically, this is how we meet Jesus again and again: through a friendship that requires presence and solidarity as its criteria. It also means joining Jesus in the breaches, with the intention to heal the disconnections that divide.

Tracing Our Life-Giving Entanglements

People inhabiting neighborhoods are not as far away from one another as they might think. Whether near or far, seeking shalom can connect our neighborhoods to heaven's priorities, even the dreams of the prophets. Dr. King wrote from the neighborhood of Birmingham, "I am cognizant of the interrelatedness of all communities and states. . . . We are caught in an inescapable network of mutuality, tied in a single garment of destiny. Whatever affects one directly, affects all indirectly."[6]

Dr. King's "single garment" metaphor illustrates how we are not siloed from one another. We can try to isolate ourselves, but even then, we remain enveloped as part of God's larger ecosystem. Dr. King had uncanny insight into the nature of this web of mutuality, an extension of God's ecosystem and God's reign. In this web, "what affects one directly, affects all" within an "inescapable network." Even when we believe we are acting in isolation, we are connected to a host of exchanges and interactions.

In light of this, when we consider the church in mission, there are multiple ways the church can be faithfully present in a neighborhood. For one, the church is the *ekklesia*, a community gathered, Christ's presence through the collective existence of churches around the globe. The church is also represented in the different parts of the body (individuals and families) spread throughout neighborhoods, called to live the gospel intently on a daily basis. And the church is represented by brick-and-mortar institutions, which can be valuable for engaging larger governing systems in a neighborhood. Furthermore, institutions can provide a sense of presence and place in ways that individuals cannot. These three dimensions of the church in the ecosystem can impact a neighborhood at different levels.

Micro, Mezzo, Macro Entanglements

The field of social work can provide further perspective on how the church comprised of individuals, as a collective presence and even as an institutional presence, can operate in place. Social work teaches that people are entangled in neighborhood life as individuals who interact on personal levels (micro exchanges) with other individuals. Groups and institutions operating together in a neighborhood would be considered an example of mezzo-level exchanges. And when people, groups or institutions, participate at a policy and governance level, this represents macro-level engagement. If the church were to disciple people around how justice is initiated on these multiple levels, then it would be able to harmonize the different parts of the body to engage multiple parts of the ecosystem. The church could also be strategic and specific in its approaches.

Micro-, mezzo-, and macro-level engagements and exchanges happen every day in our neighborhoods. For example, on her walk to the food market, Lynn, a member of Elements Church in the South Bronx, meets someone on the corner who is in need. Lynn asks their name and introduces herself, then offers to buy them a meal (micro).

After purchasing the meal, she stops at the local food mart to purchase a pack of skinless chicken thighs for her son's birthday barbecue. She shops locally because her church taught her that doing so is an act of eco-stewardship. Lynn chooses to pay a higher price than she would pay at a large chain store because she knows her dollars would dissipate in corporate coffers at the larger store, but shopping small and local would make more of a positive impact on local business. Lynn then invites people in her church's small group along with some of her neighbors (mezzo) for some BBQ grilled chicken thighs.

After some laughs and fun, people feel more settled in the space that Lynn is hosting. Lynn's cousin Max suddenly shares how he is between jobs as an educator. He loved teaching high school science for a few years in the charter school system but felt restricted by the school's culture when it came to introducing new ideas. Jim, one of the small group members, hears this and shares with Max how he works for an organization named Urban Strategies, which recruits talented teachers for its inner-city schools. Max and Jim exchange information before the night ends. Not one week later Max proceeds to submit his résumé to the organization, and a new opportunity is born to work a local public school connected to a government-funded agency called the Department of Education (macro).

One morning while Max is walking into work, he sees a church flyer announcing a backpack drive three weeks before the start of the school year in early September in New York City. These backpacks would be fully stocked for the school, which is located in the Mott Haven area of the South Bronx in the poorest urban district. This (mezzo-level) action mobilizes parishioners on a Sunday morning to buy fully stocked backpacks. The backpack drive turns out to be a success, and the church is able to engage multiple families, making their presence known in the neighborhood.

After some months on the job in the public school system, Max hears a report that the school is evicting the local church that uses its space every Sunday. The eviction is connected to a larger directive about the separation of church and state coming from city government. For some time, the pastor of the local church, Rowland Smith, and the principal of the school, Carmen Arollo, have affirmed how the relationship between school and church had been generative and mutually beneficial. The church provided school supplies and volunteers when needed and even commissioned young artists to beautify the school through the spray-painting of beautiful murals. Considering this vital connection, the church also began to strategize around overturning the new policy proposal (macro engagement).

The local church pastor, Rowland Smith, called on multiple churches to join in a protest around the "right to partner." During one of the demonstrations some of the local clergy who participated were arrested for civil disobedience, demonstrating their concern for the well-being of the local school. Ultimately, protesting against the Department of Education led to the reversal of the proposed policy to ban churches from meeting in schools. The church through its local influence was able to reverse a policy that would have unraveled a vital relationship in a school system that was underresourced.

Adopting a lens of micro-/mezzo-/macro-level thinking can

open up the church's imagination for neighborhood engagement. As the church continues to live into the rhythm of neighborhood life, it can discern and chart distinctive pathways of connection into the common life of the neighborhood.

Metaphors of Presence in Place

One of the practices I do with church planters and pastors is to discern a metaphor of presence in their neighborhoods. Just as Jesus used metaphors for the church, such as the bride of Christ, salt and light, and a city on a hill, metaphors of presence can begin to shape the church's practice of presence in a community. These are images that are emblematic of Christ's presence through his followers in the world.

Entering a metaphor of presence begins with sacred curiosity. We get to discern what faithful, humble presence will require in our specific context, according to our calling as a church. In this regard, churches will battle the temptations of coloniality. They can either choose metaphors of centeredness, seeing themselves as a "flagship" institution, or they can see themselves in some ways as part of a fellowship, within an "inescapable network of mutuality."

The church I colead has a vision for our community "to be woven together in Christ." Woven-ness animates our efforts to connect with our neighbors; we desire our neighbors to know we're present and can hopefully come to some form of connectedness with them in the common life. We see ourselves as co-weavers with them in mending some of the tattered places of East Harlem.

One way we see this weaving happen is through our partnership with an organization named Exodus Transitional Community (ETC). ETC has worked in the East Harlem Community for twenty-three years, providing services to returning citizens, people who have been impacted by the carceral system. Our church rents space at ETC for our Sunday gatherings. But our board determined our connection would go beyond a rental check. We then began to discern ways we could be more woven together with the mission of Exodus. Part of this weaving began with my bivocational work, which includes using my gifts as a trainer and consultant with Exodus. In this capacity, I have developed deep connections of trust with the staff over the years.

Being tethered to Exodus opened up doors for us to run mentoring programs for returning citizens in partnership with other East Harlem churches. We feel privileged to help provide a web of support for participants dealing with the strain of returning home after being released from prison. Our church was also able to integrate Exodus into our Sunday service rhythms. Jamel, an ETC staff member, facilitated a class on mass incarceration from the point of view of someone who has been directly impacted. Jamel held the wisdom and the expertise here. He was also instructive to our church on how to receive people who are justice impacted, saying, "We don't always want to be known as people who are justice impacted; we just want to be known as people."

Jamel contributed his gift of facilitation, and was seeking the dignity that comes with mutuality, with shalom. Cole Arthur Riley puts this into beautiful perspective when she writes, "And what is shalom but dignity spread out like a blanket over the cosmos?"[7] We realized as a church that weaving together with ETC would mean realizing that we all bring different threads to this "single garment of destiny." Our patterns of engagement with ETC are the faithful patterns we create on a small scale, allowing for the dignity of mutual contribution to be made manifest.

Harmonizing Our Efforts

Right relationship and mutuality can be a reflection of heaven in our neighborhoods. The church makes it manifest through the small daily practices of individuals, groups, or institutions. To this end Adrienne Maree Brown writes,

> How we are at the small scale is how we are at the large scale. The patterns of the universe repeat at scale. There is a structural echo that suggests two things: one, that there are shapes and patterns fundamental to our universe, and two, that what we practice at a small scale can reverberate to the largest scale. These patterns emerge at the local, regional, state, and global level—basically wherever two or more social change agents are gathered. . . . And this may be the most important element to understand—that what we practice at the small scale sets the patterns for the whole system.[8]

Churches that are led by the Spirit into placemaking in neighborhoods can work to cultivate patterns and practices of mutual care with their neighbors. Shaped by sacred curiosity, the church can become attuned to the interconnected nature of neighborhoods as sacred ecosystem, even giving mind to how one system in a neighborhood can impact another—for example, how neighborhoods are still impacted by a history of redlining practices, or how school systems with a higher income bracket will have more resources.

The church can further reimagine its presence by discerning which powerful metaphors can point it to faithful presence in a place—one that sees the flourishing beyond Christians in the neighborhood, into a flourishing for the whole beloved community. In the spirit of Dr. King's "inescapable network of mutuality," where what affects one can affect all.

How can we as the church, then, mindfully engage our ecosystems on micro, mezzo, and macro levels? Perhaps these approaches can expand our thinking about discipleship, with the hope that we can become living embodiments of shalom at every level of society. The irony of this pursuit of peacefulness and harmony will mean a simultaneous pursuit of justice, with righteous demands. As Frederick Douglass once wrote, "There is no progress without struggle."[9] Right relationship, then, as we will discuss in the following chapters, requires that a form of Jubilee justice continually circle back to challenge and transform larger systems and their processes.

INTERLUDE

A HEALTHY NEIGHBORHOOD

Economic justice in the neighborhood ecosystem—that's the goal. But what does that look like?

One of the great joys of our work has been the people we know trying to practice theologically informed, neighborhood focused, economic commitments. Unsurprisingly, the way those commitments play out in practice always look a little different. But each group in its own way is trying to answer the same question: What does economic justice look like in the neighborhood ecosystem?

Sometimes it looks like organizations that have developed city blocks worth of economic development projects. Sometimes it looks like groups taking a block-by-block approach to housing and community revitalization. Sometimes it looks like small social enterprises that target particular populations of people in the community. Their projects and initiatives look different, but they represent a shared commitment to enacting just expressions of economic life in the neighborhood.

Of course, there is no formula to cultivating a just and flourishing economic ecosystem, but we can learn a lot from others who are experimenting. The framework we discuss in parts 2 and 3 is our attempt to build on what we are learning and expand our collective imagination for what is possible. Before unpacking that gleaning-Sabbath-Jubilee framework, though, we want to pause and offer a few initial reflections on helpful principles that can give us a different way to answer the question, What does economic justice look like in the neighborhood?

Envisioning just economic lives in the neighborhood doesn't have to mean prescribing certain projects to produce certain outcomes. The temptation would be to define a set of outcomes and try to achieve them in every community. That is not our approach. Instead, we want to try to identify certain characteristics that evidence the kind of healthy economic ecosystem we desire. In that sense, if these characteristics are present and growing in the neighborhood, we can feel confident that we are moving in the right direction. Those characteristics are participation, mutuality, and resilience. Our contention is that we can evaluate the effectiveness of the gleaning-Sabbath-Jubilee framework in action based on the extent to which these three characteristics are growing, because they help cultivate a climate that allows for the entire ecosystem to flourish together.

Learning from Wendell Berry

I (Adam) owe a debt to Wendell Berry. Not only because his writing is beautiful and prophetic, but also because he has helped me see in new ways, which is essential to the work of justice. Wendell Berry—even writing from a largely agrarian view—is a gift to those of us trying to envision just economic ethics for the neighborhood ecosystem.

Thinking theologically about economic ethics, Berry interestingly says that one could define the perfectly just economy as the "kingdom of God."[1] By referring to the kingdom of God as an ideal vision for economic life, he is searching for a term big enough to encapsulate everything he sees contributing to the flourishing of an ecosystem/neighborhood. His intuition to say that economic vitality and a healthy neighborhood are bound up together in something as grand as God's kingdom is worth noting.

Berry acknowledges, though, that it is helpful to find ways of speaking about the kingdom of God that transcend the specifically Christian way of seeing, suggesting that "Great Economy" is one way of doing so. He writes, "The human economy, if it is to be a good economy, must fit harmoniously within and must correspond to the Great Economy; in certain important ways, it must be an analogue of the Great Economy."[2] In other words, in organizing our economic life together, we ought to take our cues—so far as we have learned to discern—from the ideal conditions laid out for us in the theological vision of God's kingdom.

The ideal of God's kingdom governing our economic life means that the exchanges of an economic system in neighborhood life are not value neutral—they all paint a picture of the ethics we embody. They are a true barometer of the relative justice of our life in community. The goodness of our economic life is not relative or open to self-determination because the kingdom of God / Great Economy sets standards for all that is good, right, and true. Berry hits the nail on the head when he says, "We seek the Kingdom of God . . . by our economic behavior, and we fail to find it if that behavior is wrong."[3]

At the same time, it would be naive or arrogant to suggest that we can enact the full intentions of God in community. No creative business project or affordable housing initiative will ever fully realize the kingdom of God. That's not what the work is doing to begin with. Even though we cannot enact everything of the kingdom of God, it is incumbent upon us to do what we can, no matter how small in the scope of things. Instead, those small things point, or give expression, to the larger vision of the ideal of the kingdom of God. That reality does not excuse us. It gives shape to our pursuits. Instead of thinking we can enact God's kingdom, we must follow Berry's lead as he calls our attention to the little or local economy— that is, the "narrow circle within which things are manageable by the use of our wits."[4]

That narrow circle is the field of view of this book. The systems and structures of global economies will not rise and fall because of the work of ordinary folks in normal neighborhood spaces. But the tactics we explore in this book take seriously the charge to tend to the spaces in front of us and, perhaps more significantly, are an attempt to honor the dignity of those who are ignored in the boardrooms of the global economy. This is a more concrete way of conceiving of life in community and a better way to cultivate a healthy neighborhood ecosystem. It is fundamentally more human.

Tending to the local economy as a first priority is a choice to live more humanly, economically speaking. Berry puts it plainly: "For a human, the good choice in the Great Economy is to see its membership as a neighborhood and oneself as a neighbor within it."[5] In the global economy, the particularity of people and places can get erased—which can abstract inequity into issues we can hold at arm's length. We might, in turn, default to charity only because we don't see concrete paths toward societal change. Real vitality in the ecosystem will require much more than the charity industrial complex we see all around us. As Berry says, "To help each other . . . we must go beyond the coldhearted charity of the 'general good' and get down to work where we are."[6] We want this book to push our imaginations to envision creative ways to get down to work where we are.

Participation, Mutuality, and Resilience

Thus, we turn to the three characteristics of increasingly healthy neighborhood ecosystems—participation, mutuality, and resilience. With the backdrop of the Great Economy, Berry helps us to think through those characteristics.

Participation

The first characteristic of a healthy neighborhood ecosystem is *participation*. In the following chapters, we will look at various ways people, and entire populations, are excluded and overlooked in the status quo of economic life in community. Participation challenges the exclusion of those considered "the least" and invites us to value the real diversity of the ecosystem.

In many of the communities we have in mind as we write,

scores of people are left out and many pockets of the population are overlooked, considered too insignificant to bring benefit to the community. But Berry writes, "One of the principles of an ecosystem is that diversity increases capacity. . . . A little economy may be said to be good insofar as it perceives the excellence of these benefits and . . . preserves them."[7] Berry's deceptively simple observation of the value of diversity in an ecosystem challenges the forces that seek to exclude those who do not fit the mainstream definitions of value and potential.

These insights come into clearer view the more we allow our imaginations to be shaped by the nature of life in the ecosystem. For example, one of the fundamental ideas José unpacked in chapter 2 is that ecosystems invite us to take the relationship *between* things seriously. As Berry writes, "The first principle of the Kingdom of God is that it includes everything; in it, the fall of every sparrow is a significant event. . . . Everything in the Kingdom of God is joined both to it and to everything else that is in it."[8] Ecosystemic thinking beckons us to consider the *in between*, the connections—or lack thereof—among the diverse component parts of the community, and wonder together how we might strengthen existing connections or dismantle those things that block the *betweens*.

If there is a baseline interconnection among everything in the ecosystem, that means that each participant in the ecosystem is valuable, and also that we come to understand the value of each participant only in relation to the other parts. It also means that nothing is autonomous or free to think of itself as self-sufficient. Here, we hear echoes of the apostle Paul chastising the church in Corinth (1 Cor. 11–12), as some among them had come to believe they could function outside of this communal reality.

So how do we value participation? To start, local economic participation means that neighborhood life is, as much as possible, locally led. Individual people need to be particularly engaged in the economic systems that determine local practice. Local determination of economic practice is unusual in our modern day. Instead, today "our major economic practice . . . is to delegate the practice to others."[9] Our economic fortunes are largely determined by forces well outside the locale in which we live, making the health of local ecosystems dependent on outside determinations.

Finding ways to counter those external forces is essential to neighborhood life. Wendell Berry sees people working against those forces as they "find ways to shorten the distance between producers and consumers, to make the connections between the two more direct, and to make this local economic activity a benefit to the local community."[10] The more interactive the economy, the more neighbors can determine their economic fortunes together. Valuing local participation in economic life is a way of redistributing power dynamics, often between rich and poor. Such practices "give everybody in the local community a direct, long-term interest in the prosperity, health, and beauty of their homeland."[11]

Participation also helps communities value the unique potential and value of individual people. Celebrating the value of each neighbor is a demand the kingdom of God places on us.[12] Prioritizing participation enables us to equate individual participation with the notion of contributive justice. That is, to value the unique contributions of individual neighbors is to take seriously the notion that God has endowed each person with a particular set of skills, dispositions, and perspectives that are, at face value, a gift to the world—what, in the Christian tradition, we might call *vocation*. This is, in Berry's mind, an issue of justice. Quoting art historian and philosopher Ananda K. Coomaraswamy, he notes the critical need that "each member of the community should perform the task for which he is fitted by nature. . . . The two ideas, justice and vocation, are inseparable."[13] A healthy ecosystem is characterized by individuals participating in ways marked by their gifts and passions. In doing so, local economies can proclaim Great Economy realities.

So, in our minds, having a value for participation begins well before any actual "work" takes place. It starts with a serious commitment to integrating into normal, everyday neighborhood life. No doubt, many of you reading this consider this observation obvious to the point of being nonsensical. But in our experience, too often people of faith with good hearts and excellent intentions fail at this very point, which hamstrings the work long term. This was one of the problems with the pie shop experiment. The idea *came from outside the community to the community*. It is very difficult to truly express a value for participation in that regard.

Instead, a better approach would be to begin as a neighbor. Seeing our futures as bound up with the futures of our neighbors means that we "begin" our commitment to seeking economic justice in the neighborhood as one belonging to a community (see the following "Mutuality" section). As a neighbor committed to economic justice, my first role might be as a listener. What concerns are people naming? What hopes are they sharing? What fears or obstacles are people facing? What are the threads and points of connection? Who is already trying some things?

From there, we can convene. One of the best examples of groups valuing wider participation are those who convene the community for conversation and ideation. Examples of this are popping up everywhere (some of which we highlighted in our previous books).[14] Convening regular gatherings where neighbors can share ideas and vision for the future helps us work together as neighbors rather than as people of faith doing our own thing as we sometimes do. These are spaces where we should expect to share in the wisdom of the community, to notice the priorities of the people, and to witness the natural leaders of the neighborhood arise. Allowing the neighborhood (which we are part of!) to set the agenda, priorities, practices, and more is more in line with the value of participation than the usual practice of church and nonprofit in community.

Good conveners are very often emerging community organizers as well. It may well be that my role in community is to connect the "players" and facilitate the work springing from those connections. I might leverage my connections and networks, but I assume others have connections and networks we will need connections to as well. Each of us have experiences and relationships that can help us foster health in the neighborhood ecosystem. Participation as a growing characteristic in the neighborhood will mean that the work we do will be more and more a product of the people.

Mutuality

This leads us to the second characteristic of a healthy neighborhood ecosystem: *mutuality*. The same way the underground network of an ecosystem shares resources to ensure the health of the whole, Berry speaks to the "practice of neighborhood" by which "neighbors ask themselves what they can do or provide for one another, and they find answers that they and their place can afford."[15] Practitioners in the stream of Christian community development might echo these sentiments, appealing to texts like Jeremiah 29, which suggests the essential need for individual people to understand the very normal and ordinary ways their lives are tied up with their neighbors' lives and with the overall health of the neighborhood. An "us versus them" mentality will hinder a community from flourishing. A healthy neighborhood is always developing a sense of common story and identity that combats the adversarial nature of so many human relationships. An extended quote from Berry's "Two Economies" is worth consideration:

> Competitiveness cannot be the ruling principle, for the Great Economy is not a "side" that we can join nor are there such "sides" within it. Thus, it is not the "sum of its parts" but a *membership* of parts inextricably joined to each other, indebted to each other, receiving significance and worth from each other and from the whole. One is obliged to "consider the lilies of the field," not because they are lilies or because they are exemplary, but because they are fellow members.[16]

A few observations: First, the Great Economy champions mutuality by refusing to allocate worth to the relative size of one's economic engagement. Second, the Great Economy encourages mutuality because the economic realities of those on the margins affect the entire community. Third, the Great Economy contrasts mutuality with the "winner take all" of modern economic norms with a vision of an interconnected, interrelated community of members whose economic fortunes are tied together. Lastly, each person's inherent value is celebrated—like a lily of the field, full of beautiful fruit and potential—each one an essential part of the ecosystem. Practically, one cannot take Berry seriously and not come to the conclusion that at the neighborhood level *we are all in this together.*

One of the more interesting ways we witness people leaning into mutuality is through hyperlocal business development projects. We will point to a few of these throughout this book, but one example in my (Adam's) community that is certainly happening elsewhere is the creation of hubs that prioritize local business owners. In one small city block, an organization is running a number of economic development projects, but it is also creating ways for local owners to build their own business ventures. There's a Black-owned bookshop, and some local growers show up in the parking lot for an informal farmers market while a pop-up food vendor prepares meals. A local housing developer bought an abandoned factory to use as a local business incubator, and a plant shop owner has a vision for serious connection to the neighborhood. These examples have varying degrees of explicit focus on the neighborhood ecosystem itself, but each contributes to a vision for how cultivating hyperlocal business ventures can improve the overall health of the neighborhood. We will see how these projects create, or don't create, any long-term fruit in the ecosystem, but even in these nascent stages, we observe a commitment to mutuality and a recognition of the possibilities for a neighborhood when we take our interdependence seriously.

Resilience

This neighborhood mutuality leads to the third characteristic we want to explore, *resilience*. In general, resilience is "the capacity to cope with [life-changing crises]. . . . Resilience . . . is not avoiding and denying, but accepting, surviving, moving on and growing."[17] When we talk about resilience in the neighborhood ecosystem, we are thinking of the entire community's ability to handle difficult situations. In the communal context, resilience is the ability of the "social system" to "deal with disasters and devastation without going under and, more importantly . . . mitigate the effects of the calamity by implementing restorative procedures effectively."[18] The neighborhoods that are in our mind as we write are often faced with innumerable challenges and, as such, face serious adversity in the pursuit of health and vitality. In a crisis situation, the resiliency of a person/community is tested, but many neighborhoods experience a kind of ongoing adversity, which, if seen correctly, "can provide the fertile soil on which to cultivate resilience."[19]

That means that neighborhoods can develop resilience over time. Clemens Sedmak argues that "resilience is a skill that can be learnt and acquired, developed and strengthened."[20] It is somewhat ironic that a trait observable only in crisis can be built only outside of, and in anticipation of, crisis. In other words, you build resilience before you need it. If you wait until you need it, it is too late. (Sort of like the concept of buying insurance.) A neighborhood that is growing in resilience will be doing all manner of other things as a way of building up the capacity to navigate adversity and crisis.

Of course, for our purposes, we are concerned about the

economic layer of resilience. In our globalized world, every local community's economic well-being is connected to forces and dynamics outside the community. A healthy local economy depends on a robust network of economic relationships outside the neighborhood. But, as with any relationship, problems arise when that network of relationships is unhealthy. Neighborhoods can become overly dependent on outside economic forces, which can create dynamics that leave a community in a position of extreme vulnerability.

So, in an economic sense, the more a community can care for itself, the better it can navigate the waters of economic threat. Resilience, then, might be the neighborhood's level of self-sufficiency, coupled with systems that protect those most vulnerable to economic threat. This will mean fostering a diverse local economic life rather than an economic life that is wholly dependent on external players. Berry has much to say about the development of a targeted, externally dependent mono-economy model. He writes, "A community, if it is to be viable, cannot think of producing solely for export, and it cannot permit importers to use cheaper labor and goods from other places to destroy the local capacity to produce goods that are needed locally."[21]

Of course, one of the best examples of this dynamic at work, and the serious implications for such an economic approach, are the many midwestern industrial towns that allowed a majority of their economic vitality to be bound up with global industries. Even in my community in northern Indiana, we see how local economic fortunes rise and fall with global demand, and how, even now, local communities are dependent on those outside agents for economic well-being.

Of course, those most vulnerable to economic threat are the ones most likely to be severely impacted by these changes. When factories close, lower-wage workers are the most likely to be overcome by the hardships. Even if the entire community is impacted, the wealthier folks in the community have greater means to overcome the challenges on their own, while those on the lower end of the economic spectrum face multiplied challenges. The characteristics of participation and mutuality come back into play here as we realize that the resilience of the community is a communal reality. Allowing the "poor" to fend for themselves in times of economic hardship is not an option.

Instead, a community has an ethical responsibility toward everyone in it. The ecosystem cannot thrive unless the *whole* ecosystem is thriving. Economic well-being is a matter of the health of the whole. Contrary to social norms today, individual well-being takes shape within the whole. This is one way of articulating the principle of the *common good*. Clemens Sedmak likens the common good to multiplication.[22] Many conceptions of economic growth and vitality, however, are like addition. In other words, if you have four people and one makes $100, two make $75 dollars, and one makes $0; most would say the "community" has $250. However, because the common good is like multiplication, that equation means the community has $0. That is not acceptable. "It is contrary to the idea of the common good to leave behind or write off even a single person."[23] Unless a community nurtures economic well-being for the whole and the parts together, it cannot build well-being or resilience.

To build resilience, we need to gain better understanding of the economic opportunities and threats facing our neighborhoods in real time. To that end, mapping the assets and challenges of the neighborhood through an economic lens is an essential step to fostering resilience. Scores of helpful resources are available to walk you through the process of asset mapping and SWOT (strengths, weaknesses, opportunities, threats) analysis. These projects could be helpful ways of organizing the regular community gatherings we discussed earlier. As neighbors work through a process of understanding assets, opportunities, and challenges, they open the possibility of the neighborhood responding to economic threats before they become economic crises.

Healthy economic ecosystems in local community spaces will evidence growth in participation, mutuality, and resilience. These are not growth markers that find their way onto many balance sheets, but within the Great Economy of the kingdom of God, they are of significant value and worth. Berry's wonderful lines from the novel *Hannah Coulter* find deep resonance with those committed to fostering deep economic well-being in the neighborhood ecosystem. "There is no 'better place' than this, not in this world. And it is by the place we've got, and our love for it and our keeping of it, that this world is joined to Heaven."[24] Here we encounter what we could call Berry's working theology of place: There is no better place than where I stand right now. And the kingdom of God touches down in the places we love, tend, and commit to.

PART TWO

ECONOMIC ETHICS IN THE OLD TESTAMENT

In part 2, we consider the central argument of this project, namely, that the economic ethics of Old Testament Israel not only help to shed light on the continued economic injustices plaguing our neighborhoods today, but they can also ignite our imaginations for alternative economic ways of being in community that look more like the shalom of God. The ethics of gleaning, Sabbath, and Jubilee are much more than a set of laws to follow; indeed, together they constitute a framework that helps develop healthy neighborhood ecosystems and can strengthen the kind of social ethic God had in mind in giving them to Israel in the first place.

We want to consider each in turn, using these practices to examine our current social status quo and provoke deeper reflection for more faithful and more just ways of being in the neighborhood. In part 3, we will consider some more of the practical implications coming from each of these three. Here we want to consider the theological implications on our social norms and ask hard questions about what that means for faithful economic practice today.

THREE

GLEANING: FREEING THE EDGES OF OUR FIELDS

As a pastor in New York City, I (Adam) found myself facing a deep cross-cultural learning curve. Immersed in a wildly diverse immigrant community, I witnessed the remarkable resilience of families facing all manner of challenges. Perhaps the hardest for me to wrap my brain around, though, was the incredible injustices facing children of undocumented parents.

During my time there, the political debate around the DREAM Act was raging, and the heated rhetoric had a very personal face. Our youth and children's groups were populated by many first-generation immigrant children. They were incredible kids with big dreams, full of life and laughter. I'm assuming very few of them knew the names pundits, politicians, and even their sisters and brothers in Christ were calling them. These children who lived in this nation without legal status did not grasp the lengths the powers that be would go to codify their social exclusion—in many cases to score cheap points with a swelling anti-immigrant constituency. The burden of anger I felt at the challenges they would face was nothing compared to the actual burdens facing them throughout their lives if the system went unchanged or became more exacting and punitive.

As we will see, this dynamic is nothing new. Immigrant communities face staggering challenges, not the least of which is public perception and the legislative impulse to create a society that leaves them out. This is particularly true when considering these folks' capacity to flourish economically. Because of that, our work of cultivating a thriving neighborhood ecosystem marked by participation, mutuality, and resilience invites us to pay attention to the structures and systems within communities that challenge the ecosystem's health and the individual member's capacity to thrive within it. That means we must be able to answer the question, Does the local economy (including all its structures, practices, and cultural values) work for everyone? In other words, who gets economically left out, and why?

Another way of putting this is that a significant measure for the health of the neighborhood ecosystem is access (the opposite of exclusion), or the ability for each individual member to participate in, and reap benefits from, the economic life of a neighborhood in a manner that honors and celebrates that person's unique potential and contribution to the community.[1] Inequitable access to economic life in community is a fundamental violation of God's creation order.[2] Thus, identifying the people and groups that are excluded from participation in the economy is essential justice work.

Economic exclusion is an ancient practice of the power-ful to maintain an unjust status quo of society. This is why we must also be able to move from naming those who are excluded to an honest examination of why certain people are excluded in the first place. The results of our examination will be different depending on the communities in question. Each community nurtures its own particular expressions of injustice, after all. At the same time, some characteristics of exclusion are more universal, and we should expect to find some expression of them anywhere we find people being left out of authentic participation in community. Let's consider one such characteristic now.

The Politics of Scarcity and the Roots of Economic Exclusion

In 1882 the United States passed the Chinese Exclusion Act, which was the first of many pieces of legislation aimed at enacting broad, sweeping restrictions on immigration. Chinese immigrants had been coming to the United States for decades, primarily on the West Coast to work as laborers, often help-ing to build the expansive railroad system designed to open up the West to the rest of the nation. These Chinese laborers worked for drastically lower wages than non-Chinese workers would tolerate and were essentially forced to do so because of outstanding debts back in China and those incurred to secure passage to the United States. The influx of cheap labor was a boon for business owners and those able to capitalize on the vulnerable situation in which many Chinese found themselves.

ECONOMIC ETHICS IN THE OLD TESTAMENT

However, the influx of immigrants from China also inflamed the racist notions of those who saw these laborers representing a kind of "invasion." An anti-immigrant movement began to swell, first in California, and eventually spreading to the level of federal immigration policy. By the time Chinese Exclusion was enacted in 1882, anti-Chinese sentiment had given rise to state and federal policy and even forced the renegotiation of treaties between China and the United States. The resultant policy placed a ban on Chinese immigration for decades and created needlessly harsh punishments aimed at functional deportation of legally residing Chinese immigrants already within the United States.[3]

This is but one example of America's long history of anti-immigrant rhetoric and policy. Restrictive immigration policies do not arise out of thin air. Instead, they are active responses to a rise in racist sentiments aimed at immigrants. There are, of course, countless examples of explicitly racist rhetoric used toward immigrants. Founding fathers like Benjamin Franklin wrote polemically against certain forms of immigration in explicitly xenophobic ways.[4] That thread of overt racism continues to our present day. We need not reach too far back into our history to be reminded of then candidate Donald Trump calling Mexican immigrants rapists and drug dealers/traffickers.[5]

A careful consideration of our nation's relationship to immigrants reveals a less overt but equally racist opposition to immigrants as well. Often these sentiments are framed through an economic lens and create what we could call a *politics of scarcity*. The notion that immigrants are coming here to take "our" jobs has been part of the nativist playbook from the outset. When Donald Trump outlined the key points of his aggressive anti-immigrant policies, he defended them saying, "Newcomers compete for jobs against the most vulnerable Americans and put pressure on our social safety net and generous welfare programs."[6] Despite studies showing that immigrants do not take American jobs—usually lower-income immigrants take jobs that American citizens do not want—politicians have capitalized on the economic vulnerability of working-class and poor Americans by arguing that immigrants pose an economic threat to them. A Labor Department report during George W. Bush's administration "called the perception that immigrants take American jobs 'the most persistent fallacy about immigration in popular thought.'"[7]

The economic "threat" posed by immigrants creates a cover for unjust treatment of minority groups within the United States. Historic examples include anti-Irish hiring practices; anti-Semitic rhetoric centered on economics championed by business leaders like Henry Ford; the mass deportation of Mexicans (and Americans with Mexican heritage) during the Hoover administration, enacted as a kind of economic appeasement during the Great Depression; and even family separation at the border, aggressively enacted during the Trump administration, designed to deter the legal migration of asylum seekers because of the supposed threat to our economy.[8]

This racist rhetoric aims to further alienate immigrant communities by convincing economically vulnerable Americans that immigrants pose a threat to their future prospects. Anti-immigrant movements focus on economic themes because they create a divide between vulnerable populations, pitting people groups against each other and further consolidating power in the hands of a wealthy, already powerful few. Not a mere few politicians have sewn up solid electoral victories by convincing economically vulnerable groups that they were "looking out for them" by stoking the fires of racist ideology. These powerful few sow fear and discord by promoting a politics of scarcity, convincing us that there is "not enough" to go around and these "invaders" are coming to rob what is rightfully ours. As has been said elsewhere, "Scarcity feeds resentment."[9] Nativism's cancerous effect is that it dupes us into believing that actively nurturing a fear/hatred of the foreigner is a virtuous display of patriotism. Overt violence and injustice toward the immigrant, masquerading as patriotic values, is a natural outworking of centuries of power brokers fostering a climate of fear and a society of scarcity.

Because there are scores of other examples of this kind of anti-immigrant posture in our collective history, it is easy to see why so many immigrant communities experience life on the economic margins in America. It is not a passive consequence stemming from an abstract "failure to assimilate." Rather, immigrant communities throughout our history are targets of active intentions to exclude them from authentic participation in American economic life. Reaching the shores of this nation, immigrants rarely experience a warm embrace. Instead, they encounter the closed fist of a society convinced of a fictitious scarcity, committed to maintaining their economic position by excluding all others. Tragically, this is not a problem only for immigrant communities. We see this pattern repeated in various ways across the spectrum of vulnerable people groups across our society.

Life in the Closefisted Society

Stephen Covey, best known for his work in corporate leadership, wrote about the scarcity mindset in his book *The 7 Habits of Highly Effective People*. He said, "Most people are deeply scripted in what I call the Scarcity Mentality. They see life as having only so much, as though there were only one pie out there. And if someone were to get a big piece of the pie, it would mean less for everybody else."[10]

This mentality is actively nurtured in a closefisted society, and more than merely being "scripted" to see only one pie, we are constantly barraged by the message that folks on the margins are actively attempting to steal our piece of the pie. So we hedge our assets (of any kind) against anyone or anything that might threaten them. "Protect what's mine," "Grow my wealth," "Look out for me and mine"—these are mantras and marching orders for those who succumb to the fear of scarcity. In a closefisted society, truly virtuous expressions of charity and generosity are aberrations. Instead, much of the way we've come to think about money, assets, wealth, and investments creates a functional economic isolationism.

Through this lens, we cannot clearly see our responsibility for the flourishing of others. A distorted view of "what's mine" corrupts our ability to look upon our neighbor and see their plight as our own. Yet the social ethics of God call us to chasten this obsession with "ours" by recognizing the essential responsibilities we have as part of God's larger creation ourselves. Christopher Wright notes that "there is a mutual responsibility for the good of the whole human community, and also for the rest of the non-human creation, which cuts across the idea that 'what's mine is mine and I am entitled to keep and consume whatever I can get out of it.'"[11]

When we close our fists—or, what's more, when we become closefisted people who nurture closefisted structures—we close more than our fists. It turns out that we close our eyes to the plight of the poor, we close our ears to cries for justice, and we close our souls to God. We cannot experience God's intentions for us if we actively foster a closefisted disposition. In the end, scarcity deforms our souls, rendering us incapable of deepening our participation in the abundance of God. It is a kind of prison for the person or society that buys into its fears, a prison where those in chains become participants in injustice themselves.

Opening Ourselves to God's Abundant Life

Being closefisted is, of course, the last thing God wants from us, and it is precisely the kind of bondage Jesus came to free us from. Instead of believing that scarcity is all there is, God wants us to taste and experience life lived in abundance. Jesus said in John 10:10, "The thief comes only to steal and kill and destroy. I came that they may have life and have it abundantly" (ESV).[12] Indeed, it may even be that we can confidently claim that scarcity, or the fear of someone taking what is ours, is rooted in the very identity of the enemy, or enemies, of God. Those who are the enemies of God will in fact take and destroy, but God offers a life of abundance.

Taking this one step further, Jesus's words indicate an abundant life that is filled to overflowing. This striking notion affirms the idea that God gives us more than we can use (even more abundant life than we can handle!). What do we call the extra anything that we cannot use ourselves? Margin. What an incredible thought, that God gives us so much abundant life that there will be margin, some left over!

As with the widow's oil in 2 Kings 4, God fills the jars of our lives with so much life that no stopper could contain it. It will overflow. The question, naturally, is what are we to do with the overflowing oil of life that God gives us? The person with the closed fist—enslaved to a scarcity mindset—would hoard and hide. But the scriptural story(ies) shapes our imaginations in different ways.

Consider the story of Jesus multiplying the loaves and fish in Matthew 14:13–21. Here the disciples found themselves in a situation where there was decidedly not enough. They had a genuine concern that resources were scarce, not enough to go around. What could they do? Their best suggestion was to send people away to fend for themselves. But instead of sending people away, Jesus drew the crowd to him to experience God's tangible abundance together. And what was the first thing Jesus did? He invited the most vulnerable person in the midst, a small boy, to give up what scarce resources he had. The scarcity mindset would implore the boy to close his hand to Jesus, but when the boy opened his hand, he created a way for God's abundance to flow. Everyone in the crowd—all five thousand (some scholars think this number could have been as high as fifteen thousand) people—had their fill, and guess what? Twelve overflowing baskets of God's abundance were left over.

God's abundance reveals scarcity to be a sham and invites a kind of tactile repentance for those who have profited off the injustice it creates. This is why Zacchaeus's confession was accompanied by economic restitution. A genuine encounter with the full-to-overflowing life of God will always engender concrete responses that demonstrate the liberation of those previously enslaved to scarcity.

God's abundance can be practiced. Jesus told us not to store up treasures (hoarding and hiding from others), but instead, even if our abundance is so small as to have two shirts, we ought to give away one as a demonstration of trust, an understanding that resources are never meant to stop on our block, and a belief that God can take our meager margins and create abundance for all of us to share in together.

For us to be a people who practice local expressions of economic justice as individuals, as churches, and as communities, the first step is not merely to recognize our closefisted postures but to counter those impulses, and the actions of our society, with a decidedly openhanded approach to our assets. An openhanded posture trusts in the abundance of God and is an active apologist for the freedom God's abundance makes possible in the world.

We need a pathway, guide rails perhaps, that help us imagine new ways in a society of scarcity. Fostering this way of life goes beyond the practice of charity (though it certainly includes that). We seek a posture in the world that directly confronts the injustice that grows from a societal embrace of scarcity. We desire an active resistance to fearmongering that can challenge the rhetoric of those who seek to exclude and marginalize the most vulnerable members of our society.

Enter Gleaning

The first layer of the economic model we are building together here is rooted in the Old Testament practices shaped by the gleaning laws of Leviticus 19. In that text, God told the people, "When you reap the harvest of your land, do not reap to the very edges of your field or gather the gleanings of your harvest. Do not go over your vineyard a second time or pick up the grapes that have fallen. Leave them for the poor and the foreigner. I am the LORD your God" (Lev. 19:9–10).

Advocating for thousands-year-old agricultural mandates from God as a starting point for a justice-oriented model for economic life in community might seem strange, well into the twenty-first century as we are, but hear us out. In this text, we see that the backbone of God's economic vision taking root in our communities will often begin with a shift in the posture and practice of those who hold the assets of a community. Without such a shift, the exchange of injustice for the nurturing of God's justice faces serious obstacles. Before we dive deeper into how this reshapes the character of our economics, let's take a look at the concrete actions called for by these gleaning laws and the economic effects created by their implementation in Israel's society.

Very practically, the gleaning laws were pretty straightforward, if a bit unexpected. First, landowners were not to harvest all the way to the edge of their fields. Second, they were not to "go over" the land a second time and pick up what was missed in the first harvest. These remaining crops were to be left for the poor. (Notably, the immigrant is mentioned specifically in this command.)

The idea that landowners would not harvest all their crops

but instead leave some of the harvest unharvested would have seemed foolhardy. Not only were they leaving food in the field to rot, but presumably, they were leaving profits unrealized.[13]

The edge of the field (and the second-pass gleanings) acts as a metaphor for *margin*. Logically, it would make good agricultural and economic practice to widen the margin, in case of drought, pestilence, or any other unknown factor that might impinge on landowners' ability to feed their families and make a profit.

God, however, invited landowners to consider a different possibility with their margin. Rather than viewing their margin as a way to secure their own future (something someone with a scarcity mindset would see as just plain common sense) the Lord called the landowning elites to instead free the edges of their fields as a means for creating opportunity for the poor to flourish in community. If God does in the field what God does in all the world, we should expect that when these folks freed their edges and offered God their margin, that God's abundance would flow like the widow's oil. This is what gleaning is supposed to do, create an expectation of the experience of God's abundance. At the same time, when people open their fists, believing that they have enough in a world afraid of not having enough, the practice of gleaning becomes powerfully prophetic.

Gleaning Creates Opportunity, Not Charity

Notice a couple things about these gleaning laws. First, gleaning was not optional, but a requirement of divine faithfulness motivated by divine character. This is based on the assumption that the community of the people of God would reflect the character of God in its basic life and practice. The Theology of Work Project put it this way:

> Gleaning is a process in which landowners have an *obligation* to provide poor and marginalized people access to the means of production (in Leviticus, the land) and to work it *themselves*. Unlike charity, it does not depend on the generosity of landowners. In this sense, it was much more like a tax than a charitable contribution. Also unlike charity, it was not given to the poor as a transfer payment. Through gleaning, the poor earned their living the same way as the landowners did, by working the fields with their own labors. It was simply a command that everyone had a right to access the means of provision created by God.[14]

This helps us see that gleaning deals with the question of access, directly confronting the injustice of economic exclusion. Because gleaning is not a question of generosity, we are able to see these practices as a redress of unethical behavior, a reset for a society bent out of whack by the practices of scarcity.

The gleaning laws are a way of centering the plight of the economically vulnerable, forcing those with means to consider the poor in their economic decision-making. These decisions, as the US Catholic Bishops argue, "must be judged in light of what they do *for* the poor, what they do *to* the poor and what they enable the poor to do *for themselves*."[15] Critically, the gleaning laws are designed to enable the poor to fashion their own future. Beyond a handout, the spirit of gleaning is opportunity, a critical first step for individual and communal flourishing.[16]

We will see across all three layers of this economic model God affirming the autonomy, agency, and capacity of the poor toward self-determination and freedom. Of course that is the point, because, as we have said, economic Jubilee is a *liberative vision* for the poor. The freedom for the poor to make something of the freed-up fruits of the field is embedded in the DNA of the way God creates economic opportunity. Yet poverty and vulnerability are too often framed as the result of some character defect on the part of the poor and the assumption that the poor lack the skills and/or intellect to flourish. Louise Zwick, cofounder of Casa Juan Diego in Texas, said that "in a milieu in which the possession of material goods and wealth status have become the landmark for respect, the poor are designated as failures and losers."[17] The denial of the potential and capacity of the poor is one of the great hypocrisies of our society.

We note with interest that God did not determine how the fruits of the field were to be used by the poor. God only mandated what the wealthy landowners were to do with their assets. Landowners were not benefactors in this arrangement, because the poor and the foreigner were actually fashioning their own futures. Notice that the edges of the field were not to be gathered and handed out; they were simply to be freed up. The poor and the foreigner—scriptural shorthand for the most economically vulnerable members of society—are not presumed to be without motivation and capacity. God sees the potential in the economically vulnerable to fashion a flourishing future for themselves if they are given an opportunity to do so.

We also note with even greater interest how diametrically opposed the gleaning laws are to much of what passes as economic development today, where those with assets usually dictate the terms of arrangements to those without. When the wealthy believe that the poor are, in and of themselves, insufficient to the task of building a future for themselves, it manifests in structures that allow those with assets to maintain control of their assets, even as they "give them away." We must apply our best thinking to *rethinking* our practices so as to actively resist those lies. As is always the case with injustice, it comes down to a question of who holds the power.

Gleaning Challenges Power and Paternalism

Second, by following gleaning laws, the powerful and wealthy intentionally gave up power. In other words, practicing the gleaning laws represented a loss of control by those who had it.

In our experience, this may be the hardest thing for today's version of the wealthy Levitical landowner to do. The nature of our society, so deeply shaped toward a culture of economic scarcity, trains us to resist being openhanded with our assets. In the church, we are quite used to the notion that we "owe" God the firstfruits of our labors, a tithe and offering that we give back to God out of thanksgiving for God's gifts to us. This was also rooted in Old Testament agro-economic practices. However, we have also gotten used to the notion that as long as I give my firstfruits to God, what I do with the rest of the harvest is up to me. But the gleaning laws challenge that notion of personal/societal economic autonomy by suggesting that our *last fruits* are not for us to control either.[18] Our margins are not just for us, and in giving up control of our margins for the poor to make use of—effectively making our discretionary surplus *their* discretionary income—we surrender the power over our resources that society suggests is our right to claim.

All of us have probably had a conversation about the right way to give money to a person on the street. If we had a dollar for every time we've heard someone say, "I don't give money to people on the street because, you know, *what are they gonna do with that dollar?*" well, it would likely redefine the abundance of our bank accounts. (To be honest I [Adam], have this conversation with myself all the time; as I write this, I am remembering I had this internal back-and-forth just yesterday.)

But withholding money from the poor by feigning a concern for the good and proper use of that money is not virtuous; it is a way of maintaining control. How often do our employers ask us before issuing our paychecks what we intend to do with the money they are about to give us? How often do they circle back to make sure we used it for good purposes? Of course, that notion is ludicrous. And it is a different situation as we have worked for monies now owed. But, we wonder, why does the fact that it is a so-called handout make it acceptable to exert that kind of control? Gleaning challenges the premise of a handout and that mindset over all. Surely we've never heard a rationale given that lends credibility to the notion that withholding resources from the poor is a kindness.

Exerting control in this way does, however, smack of the worst forms of paternalism that have come to shape much of what we call charity and philanthropy today. "What are they gonna do with that dollar?" is more than a question we proffer when we don't want to share our spare change. This question may actually reveal our collective social enslavement to the closed fist of scarcity.

Consider how the charity industrial complex works today. Many would-be "givers" insist on maintaining their right to dictate the terms of their philanthropy because it is *their money*. There are for-profit businesses that exist to placate the impulse of the wealthy to control the way in which their "charity" is used on behalf of the poor. As someone who has worked in various nonprofit settings, I (Adam) know how hard it can be not to center the preferences of the wealthiest donors just to keep the machine running. But doing so nurtures the worst expressions of generosity and corrupts the character of gleaning ethics because it fails to deal with the question of power and control.

Gleaning also questions more investment-minded approaches that see personal economic opportunity in the creation of economic opportunity for the poor. Nowhere in Leviticus, nor any of the economic ethics of the Old Testament have we found any evidence of there being a legitimate excuse for the wealthy to capitalize on the economic progress of the poor. Many modern "impact investing" strategies have not wrestled hard enough with the way return on investment can represent a subtly disguised power play in the form of economic extraction. We will see this more clearly when we consider the practice of Sabbath, but these gleaning laws invite us to see economic extraction as a vice that creates an insatiable desire for more.

When God said to free the edges of the field and to refuse to go over the land a second time, he was challenging the wealthy to embrace the notion of enough and to reject seeing economic inclusion of the poor as a pathway to greater economic returns for themselves. One might shirk this notion off as naive, but we contend that God meant it when commanding those "with" to give up their margins without a consideration of return. Expecting a return on investment from the poor can be just another form of exerting power over those in more economically vulnerable situations, which is fertile soil for exploitation.

Economic liberation for the poor demands a set of practices whereby the wealthy intentionally and robustly give up control of how assets are used by the poor, demonstrating the truly open hand. This is not to say we cannot be creative in creating economic opportunity. It is to say, however, that our creativity cannot be accompanied by "strings" that function as mechanisms of control by the wealthy or that cause the poor to be indebted to the wealthy.

We recognize that suggesting the wealthy have to relinquish power and control over their assets to achieve justice may seem to perpetuate the very paternalistic power structures we are writing against. Our intention is not to suggest that justice depends solely, or even initially, on the good hearts of the powerful. We agree with the famous line from Frederick Douglass that "power concedes nothing without a demand."[19] There are all manner of ways in which those in King's other America take the lead in provoking and enacting serious social change. Not only so, but expressions of economic justice can be cultivated through alternative systems (usually at a local level, which is the purview of this book).

At the same time, within a society of scarcity, where assets are increasingly concentrated (perhaps hoarded) by a comparatively wealthy few, it is not only a theological notion, but a statement of fact that a primary step required toward the *mutual* liberation envisioned in God's gleaning ethics is for asset owners to open their hands. Without a change of posture and action on the part of the powerful, the forces of injustice will continue to exert unhealthy control over the levers of society, and the theological vision of justice outlined in the scriptural tradition will remain unrealized. As Christopher Wright argues, "The law typically addresses not the poor themselves but *those who wield economic or social power.* Whereas it is common to see 'the poor' as 'a problem,' and to blame them or lecture them on what *they* must do to redeem their situation, Israel's law puts the focus instead on those who actually have the power to do something, or whose power must be constrained in some way for the benefit of the poor."[20]

The possibility of mutual liberation is what makes the ethics of gleaning so prophetic. When people committed to God's justice free the edges of their fields with no strings attached, they challenge the lie of the insufficiency of those in poverty and the very structures of scarcity that foster injustice. When asset owners let go of those assets for the sake of those experiencing economic exclusion, they confront cultural values that frame the poor (or those on the social margins) as a threat. In doing so, they extend an alternate narrative into the world that sees the economic fortunes of all as tied together, that we are indeed our sister's and brother's keeper, particularly when our sisters and brothers are under threat. Making our margin available for those on the margins to make use of as they fashion their own economic future is a mutually liberative way of life.

The ethical demands of gleaning are deeply spiritual disciplines, particularly for those of us citizens of the first America. They will expose the extent of our enslavement to a scarcity mindset. They will reveal the depth of our bias against the poor and vulnerable. They will challenge the provincial and nativist impulses in us and in our communities. They will also require courage in the face of a society committed to economically preservationist practices. They will push us into uncomfortably prophetic spaces if we commit to deepening not just our imaginations for their application but also their practice in community. They will elicit critique from those who do not see the virtue in the pursuit of God's shalom because they are addicted to maintaining power over their assets, believing that they just know better. In all these ways, and more, we should expect a robust commitment to the ethics of gleaning to challenge our formation as the people of God.

We should also expect a commitment to the ethics of gleaning to set us free to experience God's abundance in something more akin to the vision of the beloved community offered by Dr. King. We move toward this notion of abundant life in a shared community by learning to open our hands, expecting God to nurture abundance out of meager margins. If God's economic vision is to take root in our neighborhoods, if we are to see the ecosystem of our community grow healthy and flourish, we need concrete dispositions and practices to help free us from our own enslavements so that we can participate more deeply in the liberative work of God.

FOUR

SABBATH: RESTORING OVER EXTRACTING

In the early twentieth century, the Greenwood District of Tulsa, Oklahoma, was home to a flourishing Black community. The preceding decades had seen an influx of African Americans to Oklahoma as emancipation and the promise of economic opportunity—due in large part to Tulsa's oil boom—combined to establish a robust and prosperous community known as Black Wall Street. Greenwood Avenue in particular became a hub of Black business and saw the creation of significant Black wealth in the late nineteenth and early twentieth centuries.[1] This community was largely segregated from the rest of Tulsa, and while a significant number of Black folks worked in service sectors in the white Tulsa community, one of the unique features of Greenwood was its relative amount of self-sufficiency apart from white Tulsa.[2] Some compare the success of Greenwood to other more noted Black business districts in places like Chicago or Memphis.[3]

Tragically, and unsurprisingly, Black economic success raised the ire of white onlookers. Black economic vitality was a challenge to the socioeconomic status quo where Black people exist to serve the economic engines of white prosperity—be it through slavery or through low-wage menial labor as was common across the country. The status quo of white supremacy did not have room for a self-sufficient economic base within the Black community, as Greenwood represented not only a change in station for Black Tulsans but also a reordering of the social hierarchy. Hannibal Johnson, who serves on the 400 Years of African American History Commission, wrote, "The mere prospect of losing significant power and influence to African-Americans engendered a sense of dread among Oklahoma's governing elites."[4] Adding to that, the renewed sense of identity and empowerment that many Black soldiers felt returning from World War I served to magnify racial tension in communities across the United States. Tulsa was no exception, particularly related to economic matters.[5]

As Black families sought to establish themselves and create a thriving economic future, white Tulsa began to respond. "Klan activity in Tulsa during this era mushroomed. . . . Documented Klan violence in Tulsa exceeded any other city in Oklahoma during the 1921–1924 period."[6] It is interesting to note that the Ku Klux Klan names protection for states "and the people thereof from all invasion of their rights from any source whatsoever."[7] Threats against the Black community increased, including threats of violence published in local papers. The threat mentioned that Blacks must leave Oklahoma before June 1, 1921, or risk facing "dire consequences."[8]

That day saw one of the most brutal displays of violent white supremacy in the history of the United States. It would be inaccurate to call the incident, as is often the case, the Tulsa race riot. This was a massacre. Based on a false police report, a young man was arrested on suspicion of assault. The woman in question recanted her accusation as early as the day of the incident, but her recantation could not rival the momentum her false accusation created. As word spread, a crowd of white Tulsans began to gather around the jail. Some estimates suggest that by early morning on June 1, some fifteen thousand white people had formed a gargantuan lynch mob.[9]

The sheer size of this lynch mob strongly suggests that this was fueled by much more than one supposed incident between two people. Indeed, it seems that the false accusation was simply the final straw in a growing tension between the two communities in Tulsa.[10] W. E. B. Du Bois later wrote, "The colored people of Tulsa have accumulated property, have established stores and business organizations and have also made money in oil. They feel their independent position and have boasted that in their community there have been no cases of lynching. With such a state of affairs, it took only a spark to start a dangerous fire."[11]

The economic fortunes of the Black community were a bridge too far for white Tulsa. The historical record corroborates Du Bois's assessment. As whites ransacked the Greenwood District, they could be heard yelling, "These [damn] Negroes have better things than lots of white people."[12] Over the next day, whites killed dozens (if not hundreds) of Black people and burned down more than a thousand homes and businesses. A thirty-five-block area was nearly completely destroyed, creating millions of dollars' worth of damages.[13] Greenwood was destroyed. The reasons were clear.

> Resentful of the evident ambitiousness and affluence of Greenwood's upper class, fearful of the assertiveness displayed by black veterans of World War I who insistently demanded for themselves the democracy for which they had risked their lives abroad in the Great War, animated by the idea that Negroes must be made to stay in their "place" at the bottom of the social totem pole, habituated to the use of vigilante violence, and angered by (false) news reports and rumors about the rape of a white woman by a black man, white Tulsans killed at least twenty-five of their black neighbors—and probably dozens more—and torched thirty-five city blocks, rendering more than a thousand families homeless.[14]

The Tulsa massacre cannot be viewed as an isolated incident perpetrated by a group of individually violent racists. Instead, it must be seen as a natural outcome of a horrific expression of the violent economic extraction that has characterized the relationship between white and Black America from the beginning. The emerging Black wealth threatened the long-standing socio-structural system where whites freely plundered the wealth potential of Blacks. When Tulsa's Black community began to realize the economic potential they inherently possessed, that was intolerable to the protectors of the extractive system of white supremacy. Black wealth had always existed as the property of white communities, and the disruption of Tulsa's status quo was met with bloody retribution. The intersection of white supremacy and economic extraction is fertile soil for violent injustice.

Economic Extraction as a Cultural Value

Extraction operates as a kind of cultural value that expresses itself in many ways. In the first place, extraction objectifies the human person. We've seen the way extraction objectifies non-white bodies for the profit of white communities. But, of course, humanity's appetite for wealth leads to all manner of economically extractive practices that still objectify people but don't necessarily include an element of white supremacy. US labor history is littered with examples of extracting profit from vulnerable groups, such as children or immigrant populations. At the same time, many industries have practices (sweatshops, mining, minimum wage / executive pay gaps, etc.) that generate enormous wealth through unsafe conditions and inequitable treatment. Economic extraction chews people up in the name of profit as their bodies are plundered for the wealth potential therein.

Extraction also wreaks havoc on the land itself. Seeing the land as ripe for extracting profit, agricultural and industrial practices in the United States have degraded and plundered the land for generations. Mountaintop removal is a stark expression of humanity's appetite for wealth, as beautiful landscapes are leveled in the name of increasingly efficient methods of extracting fossil fuels for industrial production and profit. Similarly, one of the United States' greatest agricultural disasters, the Dust Bowl, came about, in part, due to an uncritical pursuit of yield. As farmers, many of whom were underinformed of the collateral consequences of new techniques, overtilled the soil in search of higher production, they exposed and amplified the land's vulnerability to drought. This created the conditions for the environmental tragedy that claimed seven thousand lives and displaced a quarter million people.[15]

Finally, extraction destroys communities. The destructive force extraction exerts on communities is evidenced in the intertwined narratives of suburbanization and gentrification. Suburbanization, driven by white flight, destabilized urban communities. Instead of local city neighborhoods characterized by the interplay of residential, commercial, and social space, newly created suburbs displaced the economic potential of urban spaces and channeled it outside its traditional bounds. Suburbanites commuting to cities for work returned home with the economic fruits of these cities and put them to use in ways that helped suburban communities flourish. Monies that used to fund urban institutions such as parks and schools now went toward increasingly wealthy suburbs and left inner-city communities economically decimated. Property values plummeted, local schools (cash-strapped because of declining property values) cut essential programs, and employment opportunities vanished as companies relocated to more convenient environs for their suburban workforce. These inner-city spaces became overwhelmingly non-white.[16]

These economically crippled non-white spaces became spaces ripe for a new kind of economic extraction. As David Leong writes in *Race and Place*, "Whole communities of people (almost always communities of color), who for decades had been abandoned by white flight and public neglect, were suddenly in the crosshairs of the many economic opportunists who saw the dollar signs in the dirt."[17] Leong helps us see ways that gentrification fits the long narrative of white extraction from Black bodies and communities. So it could be argued that gentrification is a "re-plunder" of Black and brown communities for the profit of largely white communities.[18] As suburban and nonlocal people saw property in largely Black and brown communities as opportunities for profit (as landlords, property flippers, or long-term residential investments), we witness the way white America views non-white bodies and communities as fertile ground for profit and extraction.

The Hidden Costs of Extraction

These stark examples are but the outward expression of the cultural value of extraction at work. To perceive wealth accumulation as an amoral pursuit enables extractive practices to shape our imaginations and order our loves in ways that corrupt our capacity for true and full human and social flourishing. Indeed, the pursuit of wealth costs us something, and those costs often take a toll below the surface of our souls and society.

In the first place, extraction leaves people, land, and communities[19] exhausted, their potential fruitfulness taken, leaving them little of the fruits of their labor by which to restore themselves. This exhaustion is common to all, a sign of the prison in which our economic values leave the rich and the poor locked up.

Surely you've encountered this in your own life, a sense that you are pushing the natural limits of health related to work, feeling pressure to perform efficiently and produce more and better results. The ease with which we fall into patterns of extracting production from our very bodies is an expression of violence itself. Twentieth-century American Trappist monk Thomas Merton reflected on this:

> There is a pervasive form of contemporary violence . . . activism and overwork. The rush and pressure of modern life are a form, perhaps the most common form, of its innate violence. To allow oneself to be carried away by a multitude of conflicting concerns, to surrender to too many demands. To commit oneself to too many projects, to want to help everyone in everything, is to succumb to violence. The frenzy . . . kills the root of inner wisdom which makes work fruitful.[20]

Merton's insight here is the way in which the violence of extraction damages our capacity to grow in wisdom and, ironically, produces less in the way of healthy fruit. When this inner dynamic extends out into the way we orient our communities, the health of the ecosystem is damaged and fruitfulness wanes.

Equating the value of our work with what we can produce cheapens the meaning of our labor. Rather than connecting our work to a deep sense of vocation—what Wendell Berry calls "the work that one chooses to do because one is called to it by Heaven or by one's natural or god-given abilities"—society increasingly drives people to forms of work that are "determined and imposed by the economy." In such a world, "any work is all right as long as one gets paid for it."[21] Questions about the kind of work we do, and find fulfilling and life-giving, are replaced by largely economic concerns, a dynamic that shapes our values and the goals of our work life.

This kind of economic view also disconnects us from community life. The transience of American society, for the rich and the poor, is thoroughly economically driven. Instead of experiencing a local life in which economic and social flourishing are bound up together in a stable and thriving relationship between people, land, and community, we have become a society in which moving frequently for economic reasons is commonplace. The more this happens, the more vulnerable we all are to economic calamity because we do not exist within a system of support and mutuality. Instead, people are left to find support wherever they can. This is often outside their local communities, like an extended family network, and those individuals depend on outside actors for financial stability.

Obviously, when generational, family economic support structures take precedence over local communities of support, people who come from families of generational wealth have an opportunity to survive economic calamity in a way others do not. The burden of economic vulnerability, then, is experienced differently depending on a person's support system. That makes living in genuine solidarity with others across the economic spectrum difficult. This is often on display when well-meaning folks from wealthy backgrounds want to engage justice work in vulnerable neighborhoods. As many of the examples we've shared so far would attest, social barriers exist between the rich and the poor. Many times those barriers can be traced back to wealthy folks' reticence to experience the economic fortunes of the neighborhood alongside their new neighbors. They know they live "above" the adversity on the ground, and so they engage differently. I (Adam) felt this acutely when I lived in New York. Our family circumstances differed from our community's in numerous ways, and those differences prevented more meaningful mutuality in the neighborhood. The barriers between citizens of the first and second America are not torn down just because a wealthy person moves into the neighborhood.

Economic extraction solidifies the social barriers between the rich and the poor and over time widens the tangible wealth gap between the two groups. Theologian and scholar Ched Myers identifies this as one of the results of "trickle up economics," or "the transfer of wealth from the increasingly *poor* to the increasingly *rich*." This dynamic leads to increasing "income polarization . . . deepening psychic and social alienation."[22] Social isolation is codified through intentional strategies that further marginalize low-income communities and cut them off from channels for community flourishing that the increasingly wealthy take for granted, or worse, protect for themselves.

The isolation we experience disconnects us from the effects of our participation in extractive systems. As our increasingly globalized world progressively disconnects us from each other in real time and place, where and how we live becomes more economically abstract. Our consumptive practices no longer force us to reckon with the means of production and the destination of the profits being generated from our economic decision-making.

For example, how many of us know the economic practices of the companies we buy from? How much does the worker at the store get paid, and does that matter to me as I patronize the shop? Who, or what, is paying the price for our obsession with low-cost goods? Do we know where our food comes from and the methods used to produce/harvest/prepare it? Does my investment portfolio include investments in, say, private prison systems, and does my moral system cosign the practices of businesses whose profit I've tied my personal economic security to?

In the end, we are participants in an economic system of which most of us are largely ignorant. We don't have to try to practice economic inequity because complicity in injustice does not require our consent or intention. That means that even our attempts to "do good" are fraught with challenges and potential missteps.

Returning to the notion of "impact investing," certainly having the desire to create social good through business and leveraging the power of venture capital have laudable elements. This represents a shift in the thinking of some who are attempting to balance profit with social responsibility. As we mentioned earlier, though, many forms of impact investment fail to deal seriously enough with the extractive impulses of an unequal society. Investing in, say, a young entrepreneur from a low-income neighborhood has real social impact potential. In that sense, it is attractive to investors with good intentions. Government-sponsored "opportunity zones" that invite mass investment, complete with tax incentives, in low-income communities highlight the attractiveness of this approach.

At the same time, investments can also put these entrepreneurs in an increased position of vulnerability, adding the social vulnerability inherent in taking on investors to the economic vulnerability of accepting start-up funds. Even as wealthy investors bankroll the business, the real comparative risk is not authentically felt by the investor. As it becomes socially acceptable, or perhaps even socially celebrated, to look for economic opportunity in low-income spaces, we worry that the long-term results will be akin to the Old Testament dynamics these economic laws were written to address: disconnected elites holding debts over the poor and extracting profit in the name of the terms of the deal. Rather than true liberation, impact investment can lead to further economic injustice. It does not have to, though, and we will return to discussion on ways of investing in the economic fortunes of low-income communities in a later chapter.

Certainly entrepreneurs need partners in their ventures. In that regard, we are all for serious investment in entrepreneurs, particularly from communities historically excluded from participation. Investing with a desire for social impact is not actually the problem. But we believe we need to keep pushing our approach, because if our attempts to right the wrong of *exclusion* (think gleaning) inadvertently create a system of *extraction*, we will have traded one expression of injustice for another.

We therefore need systems of investment that mitigate the potential for extraction. We need a new way of framing the economic opportunity, where investment is about shared flourishing rather than individual wealth accumulation. We need a way to champion economic flourishing that also resists or rejects extraction in practice and as a cultural value. That is where Sabbath comes in.

Sabbath: Pushing Back against Extraction

We believe a robust commitment to Sabbath ethics allows communities to prophetically resist extraction, creating the possibility for the meaningful restoration of the people and places wrung dry by the practices of plunder to which we have become accustomed. We are interested in understanding what Sabbath expects from us and how a right-sighted vision for it might lead to new ways of being so that something more akin to God's justice might take root in our midst.

Along the way, we have seen the impact extraction takes on people, land, and communities. This grouping is intentional. The relationship between individuals, the place they live, and the society animated by particular people in a particular place is a reflection of the ecosystem discussed in chapter 2. The health of the overall ecosystem is going to be evidenced by the degree of harmony between each of these three in relation to the other two. In *Becoming a Just Church*, Adam unpacked this same notion related to the Trinity, where each member of the Trinity exists in harmony with the other two, and while each can be understood to a degree in isolation, the truest sense of God is only as Trinity. As bearers of the *imago Dei*, people find a deeper sense of identity through social relations. As religious education scholar Maria Harris says, a "person, by definition, means someone in connection."[23] Those connections are a reflection of the harmony between people but also extend beyond the human community. It's critical to see that the health and vitality of people, land, and communities are bound up with the others and something of the identity of each informs our understanding of the others as well. As we said earlier, the health of the overall ecosystem is interrelated. For harmony to exist for one, it must exist among all three together. This is what indigenous communities, and theologians like Randy Woodley, refer to as the "harmony way," a recognition that "all people and things are related to each other. . . . Harmony or balance is the key to all happiness, health and well-being."[24]

On the other hand, to damage the health of one area is to damage the whole. Extraction from one has consequences in the others. Theologian Richard Lowery highlights the connection between extraction and a breakdown in shalom, saying, "Economic inequality also threatens the ability of the ecosystem to sustain human life. Unrestrained consumption at the top of the economy turns vast quantities of natural resources into unusable and irretrievable thermal energy, while producing more garbage and other pollution than the natural environment can process in the foreseeable future."[25]

The practice of Sabbath is the work of cultivating restoration in the people, land, and communities broken down by the violence of extraction. It is a recognition that God's good intentions are corrupted over time and are in need of repair and a reestablishment of the harmony that characterized God's creation at the start. Woodley notes how indigenous peoples have sensed the importance of dealing with these breakdowns: "Any system, starting out fairly good (whether from small systems like a family to large complex systems, like a whole culture), can become corrupted over time. Primal peoples understand this concept, and in order to maintain harmony they embed renewal and cleansing ceremonies in their systems."[26] Sabbath has always had similar aims: renewing social relations and cleansing the impurities that have corrupted our ability to produce fruitful ecosystems of harmony between people, land, and communities.

A Weekly Practice

The earliest expression of Sabbath we have in Scripture is found in the very first chapter of Genesis as God *rests* after the work of creation is finished. Genesis 1 is essential to our overall picture of Sabbath for it roots the practice of Sabbath in the identity of God and as a model for emulation.

For example, it is unlikely God chooses rest because he is tired. In other words, Sabbath rest is not designed, initially, for recuperation. Instead, God rests immediately after the proclamation that creation is *tov meod*, or very good. Sabbath is "God's cosmic "Wow!""[27] Theologian and ethicist Norman Wirzba says, "The experience of delight is what Sabbath is all about."[28] In that sense, Sabbath rest is a celebration of the very good creation of God, a straightforward confession that creation lacks nothing, that it is enough.[29]

The ancient Judeo-Christian practice of a weekly Sabbath is meant to reflect this joyful recognition of God's "enough."[30] The word *enough* functions in several ways in our common usage. On the one hand, enough can be used in the sense of being adequate, a bare minimum, the way a teacher might tell a poorly performing student that they have done just enough to pass the course. *Enough* in this usage leaves everyone wanting more. This is the great temptation for us when we consider

God's *enough*. Perhaps best expressed in Israel's refusal to take just what they need of the bread and manna in the wilderness and always to be looking for more on the Sabbath (a sad expression of the value of extraction), humanity often intuits God's *enough* as a bare minimum requirement that leaves us wanting more than what God has given. To look at what has been given us, and to find it inadequate, fosters a desire for more—the seedbed of extraction.

Alternatively, *enough* also carries with it a connotation of abundance. This is the sense in which we might say, "Come join us for dinner; we have enough for everyone!" In saying *enough* here, we do not mean that you and we all will go away hungry. We say *enough* to signal a joyful abundance. Jesus put this sense of *enough* on display in the story we referenced in chapter 3, when basketfuls of food were left after everyone had their fill. There was enough for everyone! It bears repeating that when we think of God's *enough*, we are called to embrace the abundant reality of God's *very good* creation. God does not leave us wanting more.

Thus, the weekly Sabbath is rooted in the celebration of God's abundance. Sabbath rest is not, in the first place, about recuperation, but about the jubilant proclamation of God's *enough*. This is why we can say with confidence that Sabbath is a direct challenge to the values of extraction. We do not, like Israel in the wilderness, have to extract more than what God gives.

However, because we live in a world where harmony has been corrupted and values like extraction are deeply ingrained in us, Sabbath does indeed take on elements of holy recuperation and restoration. Weekly Sabbath recalibrates our impulse to extract as much profit potential as possible from our own bodies by inviting us to say "enough is enough" in a way that points us to remember the joyful abundance of God. This weekly practice of Sabbath trains our character toward the embodiment of our belief in God's abundant enough, which creates the conditions for us to better recognize places where harmony is threatened and to have the vision and courage to do something about it.[31]

Moving from extraction to restoration creates new possibilities for people. Rather than fostering an obsession over more (profit, production, etc.), Sabbath ethics foster a worshipful delight in God's abundance. It invites us to echo God's pleasure in creation, calling out *tov meod* as we relish our place in the ecosystem of God's creation.[32] It invites us to see refraining from work as something more than stopping, to view rest as a prophetic act of celebration of the ways in which God provides.[33] Because we are so prone to distrust God's enough, we are surely to be people who have ingrained patterns of extraction that are exhausting us and contributing to a lack of flourishing of people, land, and community. The disciplined restraint of Sabbath counters the indulgence of extraction in our day-to-day life and practice.[34]

Sabbath also reshapes our identity in light of God's restorative work. God explicitly connects Israel's Sabbath laws to their identity as a people, "a people rescued and redeemed by God,"[35] in Deuteronomy 15:15, saying, "Remember that you were slaves in Egypt and the LORD your God redeemed you. That is why I give you this command today." Myers notes that this is significant, because the Israelites were slaves to a nation that forced them to build "store cities" in which to store Egypt's excessive wealth. Israel literally built the storage facilities for the profit plunder of Egypt and the egregious indulgences produced by Egypt's extraction. God reminds the people, *I set you free from that; do not become that kind of people yourself.* Likewise, if these Sabbath ethics are meant to set us free from the pull of profit extraction today, we do well to remember that that liberation is a work of God's redemption and restoration. Sabbath sets us free to experience and participate in God's restorative work. In that sense, the weekly Sabbath was a liturgical reminder aimed at the spiritual formation of a people.[36]

A Social and Ecological Restoration

The ethics of Sabbath go well beyond the familiar weekly rhythm, though. As Exodus 23, Leviticus 25, and Deuteronomy 15 outline, Sabbath had a regular seven-year rhythm that shapes our pursuit of economic ethics for the neighborhood.

The Sabbath year defined Israel's relationship with the land. Each field was to lie fallow one year in seven.[37] In demanding that the land go unplowed and unplanted one year in seven, God was inviting Israel to see the land, and the needs of the land, as mirroring their own—a sign of the essential connection between people and place. A fallow field is a proclamation of God's enough. A fallow field is also recuperating from its overuse as landowners, in all likelihood, extracted more from the land—in pursuit of yield and profit—than the land could healthily produce. This creates a situation in which the land is vulnerable to the demands of an extractive society. Sabbath ethics call for a restoration for the land itself.[38]

The fallow field connects the practice of gleaning and the ethics of Sabbath. As the two come together, we see God's vision for the people to move from tightfisted extraction to openhanded, joyful proclamation of God's abundance. This joyful proclamation is not a private spiritual exercise; rather, it has real economic and social consequences where the rich forsake profit for the sake of the prosperity and flourishing of the poor.

The Sabbath year also aimed to redefine social relations, a safety measure meant to reestablish or solidify the harmony of a particular community. This was done through the demand for debt release (Deut. 15). The Sabbath year called for the near-total[39] practice of debt forgiveness. This included freeing those who had become indentured servants or enslaved due to debt in those years. Whatever debts had been incurred during the previous six years were released, irrespective of when the debt was incurred. In fact, to make sure the wealthy didn't close their fists to the poor, specific provisions prohibited lenders from refusing to loan in the years leading up to the debt release.[40]

Debt release is a declaration that enough is enough.[41] The nature of these debts, usually incurred by taking loans in emergency situations or when needed just to get by, create a situation for the rich to profit off the plight of the poor. Lending to the overwhelmingly poor is a small risk for the wealthy but an opportunity to profit from the poor's social location. These ancient "opportunity zones" ensured that the status quo of wealth inequality stayed firmly intact. However, when these wealthy debt holders release that debt, they are embracing the reality of *enough*, which interrupts the extractive movement of profit from the poor to the rich. This allows the poor to recuperate from their years of loss.

Debt release, because it sets the debt-enslaved free, is also an act of liberation. When the rich accept the notion of enough, the poor experience liberation. As we saw in our discussion of gleaning, for these economic ethics to produce liberation, the rich must accept reality as declared by God and embrace that reality in their economic practices. When the rich refuse to accept the joyful abundance of *God's enough*, they continue to bind the poor in the chains of their debts. Releasing debts, practicing an openhanded posture toward the poor, creates opportunity for the poor to experience economic and social restoration.

Even more, God does not intend debt release to be merely a blank slate. In place of debt, God demands the sharing of abundance. The mere elimination of debt is good, but it does not deal with the conditions that created the person's debt in the first place and does not solve the problem of their overarching economic vulnerability (which makes them likely to need emergency loans again). Instead, the debt release is to be accompanied by a parting gift of wealth. Consider the following from Deuteronomy 15 related to both those released from their debts and those released from indentured service.

> If anyone is poor among your fellow Israelites in any of the towns of the land the LORD your God is giving you, do not be hardhearted or tightfisted toward them. Rather, be openhanded and freely lend them whatever they need. . . . And when you release them, do not send them away empty-

handed. Supply them liberally from your flock, your threshing floor and your winepress. Give to them as the LORD your God has blessed you. (vv. 7–8, 13–14)

God explicitly contrasts the posture of hardheartedness and tightfistedness with openhanded generosity. The command of verse 14 to "supply them liberally" with livestock, food, and wine literally means "to hang a necklace," a stirring image of a joyful gift coming from the abundance of wealth from their stores.[42] It is the responsibility of the lender to mirror the abundance of God in their generosity toward their now former debtors. The lender acknowledges their debtors have paid back enough, they refuse to take more, and they mark the release by sharing from the enough of their table.[43] In doing so, God reveals that they are emulating the intentions of God, who has done the same for them. Interestingly, Jesus drew on this relationship between our identity as debt-released to our obligation to be debt releasers as he taught us to pray, "Forgive us our debts, as we also have forgiven our debtors" (Matt. 6:12).

In this sense, the Sabbath maintains God's preference for the poor and vulnerable. The Old Testament ethical codes surrounding the practice of Sabbath support this prioritization of the poor.[44] "Sabbath is meant to revitalize the most vulnerable workers in the household economy—the slave, the resident alien, and, first of all, the farm animals."[45] Lowery isn't equating enslaved people, immigrants, and animals in terms of identity, but he is noting the commonality of these groups as vulnerable to extraction by the powerful. A preference for the poor protects the economically vulnerable from harm, intended or otherwise. This is also why there was a ban on lighting fires on the Sabbath. It was not an arbitrary law, but a way to make sure that those in charge of household work (likely women) were not forced to work to serve the wishes of those who could afford to refrain.[46] In this sense, "Sabbath is the great equalizer. Sabbath justice begins in the home but is the basis of a much broader social ethic."[47]

This vision for a broader social ethic rooted in concern for the poor and those likely to be exploited provides a lens through which Jesus's squabbles with Pharisees over the Sabbath can take on deeper meaning. Consider the encounter in Matthew 12 where Jesus experienced antagonism for plucking grain from a field on the Sabbath (gleaning?). In defending those actions as part of the divinely inspired social ethic, he invoked the image of helping a distressed animal on the Sabbath. In both cases, Jesus defended the broader point that Sabbath commends concern for the poor—be it hungry strangers or defenseless animals.

Later on Paul would chastise the Corinthian practice of the Lord's Supper in 1 Corinthians 11. He invoked the concern God shows for the manual labor class (those forced to work while the owners got drunk on wine) and essentially called their practice a defamation of the Lord's Table. The New Testament nuance does not overlook the tangible social implications for the people of God called to prioritize the well-being and full participation of the poor. Paul echoed the critique leveled against the people of God by the Old Testament prophets for their abuse of the ethics of Sabbath, which were meant to provide inclusion, not exclusion, of the poor. Lowery notes, "This prophetic critique makes clear that Sabbath has a distinctively economic dimension. It is a matter of justice, not simply a pious holiday. In fact, the failure to attend to the needs of the vulnerable negates the value of "technical" observances of sabbath-day rest. Sabbath without justice is blasphemy."[48]

Sabbath Restoration for People, Land, and Community

The threefold nature of these Sabbath ethics points us toward God's intentions where joyful restoration replaces violent extraction. This is the movement of God's economic vision, and the pursuit of economic justice requires attending to this.[49] As we move from violent extraction toward joyful restoration, we see how the ecosystem finds balance and harmony. Sabbath turns the logic of scarcity-fueled profiteering on its head, inviting us to proclaim God's abundance through restraint and self-discipline.[50]

When wealthy landowners rest from work one day per week, they also allow their laborers the opportunity to rest and celebrate. This practice censures any movement toward unjust treatment of workers and exposes economic exploitation. A bold trust is fostered when fields lay fallow for a year and communities depend on what has already been produced—unlike the Israelites' lack of trust in the desert that the manna wouldn't last. When debts are released, social solidarity, a "generalized reciprocity,"[51] is nurtured, which resists the injustice that comes when the wealthy insist on total economic dominance in a society.[52] In place of the exhaustion and injustice brought on by extraction, Sabbath ethics foster the healthy harmony of the ecosystem.[53]

Imagining Sabbath for Today

What might these Sabbath ethics call from us today? We offer some practical advice in part 3, but beginning that discussion now by framing the conversation around ways Sabbath gets expressed in our day might be helpful.

For example, the ethics of Sabbath are expressed when people experience restoration by finding freedom from debts that have kept them under someone else's economic control. Even though huge swaths of our society are imprisoned by their debts, we can point to practices of predatory lending as a prime example of the values of extraction preying on the economically vulnerable. The model of predatory lending is based on maximizing profit by plundering the wealth of the poor and keeping them locked in debt for as long as possible. Sabbath economic ethics challenge that and call people of faith to proactively engage in strategies of debt relief and restoration of the economic fortunes of the poor. This means finding and/or creating alternative systems of lending, banking, and other forms of concrete economic activity that create opportunity for the poor so that their economic vulnerability is not deepened. We are reminded of the growing number of churches paying off huge debts in their communities, and of churches creating college scholarship programs. Despite their differences, both of these examples represent an investment in relieving the economic vulnerability caused by debt, in ways that challenge predatory lending models.

We see the ethics of Sabbath on display when local farmers challenge the values of large-scale agriculture. Instead of relying on methods of manipulation and environmental degradation to increase yield, more and more local farmers are focusing on production that cooperates with the naturally renewing life cycle of the land. They are conscious of the collateral consequences of their methods on other people and the larger community.

We see the ethics of Sabbath embodied by communities who promote mutuality and a sense of shared abundance instead of cooperating with systems of stratification that create economic caste systems. Unlike communities that erect barriers between rich and poor, which protect the wealth of the rich at the expense of the poor, Sabbath-rooted communities pursue a cooperative, as opposed to competitive, solidarity that brings the economic fortunes of all together.

The Tulsa massacre was the bloody fruit of extraction in our society. The wealthy laid claim to the economic growth of Black Tulsans in a way that evidenced their belief that the economic progress of the historically excluded also meant a loss of power and control for white Americans. Sabbath ethics indict any impulse to extract economic fruit from others. Sabbath calls us not only to loosen the grip we have on the assets in our control but also to embrace a celebratory affirmation of the economic restoration of others—particularly the most vulnerable. Sabbath ethics make it possible to reject the idea that others are a threat, and to champion the sense that our collective well-being (the harmony way) is of higher value than individual advancement. We are all in this together. As Jeremiah 29 makes plain, Sabbath-rooted communities recognize God's reality that when the city prospers, so, too, do the people themselves. We will examine these stories and snapshots in greater detail in part 3.

FIVE

JUBILEE: JUSTICE THAT CIRCLES BACK

On November 5, 2021, the US House of Representatives introduced legislation that would provide restitution to surviving generations of Black World War II veterans. If passed, HR 5905 would be a form of reparations addressing the federal government's role in discriminating against 1.2 million Black World War II veterans. What is more, surviving spouses and direct descendants would be eligible for "certain housing loans and educational assistance administered by the Secretary of Veterans Affairs, and for other purposes."[1]

The GI Bill was originally intended to offer home and college loans to World War II veterans returning home from the war. With this benefit, families could then pursue their American dream of obtaining a college education; they could also purchase a home, providing an asset that could be passed down to later generations. Unfortunately, while Black veterans did receive these benefits, ongoing discrimination prevented them from following the same path toward economic flourishing as their white counterparts.

In lieu of this, the *New York Times* told the story of one Black veteran named Eugene Burnett, who intended to cash in on the promise of home ownership in Long Island, New York. According to the article, "Bernice and Eugene Burnett tried over the winter of 1949–50 to buy a house in Levittown. . . . He recalls being impressed by the tract houses sprouting on a former potato field and a salesman's response to his inquiry about buying one: 'It's not me, but the owners of this development have not as yet decided to sell these homes to Negroes.'"[2]

Today Levittown is still considered one of the most segregated suburbs in the country. No accident—this was part of the legacy of redlining practices targeting Black veterans and many other Black families. Historically, this form of injustice can also be considered a form of systemic collusion. This is when different systems in the ecosystem such as government, real-estate, and education work together to put obstacles in the path of Black flourishing. W. E. B. Du Bois lamented this uphill battle faced by Black veterans, writing, "We return. We return from fighting. We return fighting."

HR 5906 is a policy that if enacted could circle back to right some of the wrongs committed against Black Americans. Partly, it is also a corrective measure that acknowledges the myth of meritocracy in our society. The long-held belief that a system by which individuals gain wealth and move into positions of success on the basis of their demonstrated abilities and merit. Throughout American history, we can trace back how economic gains for many white Americans have been framed in the language of the American success story, basically, what happens when an individual "pull themselves up by their boot-straps." What has not been reckoned with is how the story of success has historically come at the expense of Black, indigenous, and peoples of color (BIPOC) in the Americas. For the local church, these narratives are part of the fabric of neighborhood histories. Our neighborhoods today are living artifacts of this history, and just like God's creation, our neighborhoods "groan" for things to be made whole.

In this sacred endeavor, the church can draw on some of the ancient wisdom of a biblical Jubilee to learn how justice can circle back, with the church joining God's dream for a neighborhood, even a society. Following the path of Jubilee can point us back to God's corrective love for the people of Israel. We can begin to reimagine a form of economic discipleship that envisions and enacts restorative approaches to practices concerning land and labor.

Jubilee: Part of the Sabbath Cycle

Jubilee was a part of God's law addressing labor and land ownership practices, as well as debt forgiveness within the Hebrew community. And while Jubilee is narrowly observed within the context of Jewish tradition, the church would be remiss if it overlooked Jubilee, namely, how it can provide a theological lens for stewardship beyond tithes and offerings. If engaged seriously, a more robust engagement with Jubilee can help the church connect stewardship and discipleship to everyday neighborhood economics. This was an invitation God first extended to the people of Israel through the law of Moses as they inhabited a new land.

The practice of economic stewardship in the life of Israel was rooted in the law of Moses. It was a reflection of God's intention for the people of Israel to live as a liberated and just community. After four hundred years of bondage and hard labor at the hands of the Egyptians, the Israelites were given the law of Moses to be a guide to govern a free nation in the making.

Part of the preserving a life of freedom for Israel came through the establishment of a Jubilee year. Jubilee would happen after seven Sabbath cycles (as described in the introduction). Sabbath (from a Christian perspective) in our world can often be limited to the notion of self-care—a day off from normal work schedule to rest and recharge. But Scripture shows that Sabbath has more dimensions. The distinction was not just the cancellation of debt, which occurred every seven years; the distinction lay in how any land that was confiscated due to debt was to be returned to its original tribe. Additionally, fellow Israelites who were enslaved as laborers were to be made free.

God's law circled back, heralding good news reflected in this command from Yahweh in Leviticus 25:8–10:

Count off seven sabbath years—seven times seven years—so that the seven sabbath years amount to a period of forty-nine years. Then have the trumpet sounded everywhere on the tenth day of the seventh month; on the Day of Atonement sound the trumpet throughout your land. Consecrate the fiftieth year and proclaim liberty throughout the land to all its inhabitants. It shall be a jubilee for you; each of you is to return to your family property and to your own clan.

The word for "Jubilee" in this text comes from the Hebrew word *yoval*. The yoval was a horn used to make an announcements to the people. Jubilee's announcement proclaimed good news to those who were enslaved, indebted, and had lost their land due to this debt. Jubilee also ensured that the yoke of debt and servitude would be removed after a prescribed time; Jubilee as a cycle could also be a sobering reminder to those benefiting from the confiscation of land and indentured labor, signaling that a form of restitution was on the horizon. This holy reset would be an upheaval resetting the economic balances in in Hebrew society, which can also be seen as a form of social righteousness.

Jubilee as Social Righteousness

Jubilee was observed on the Day of Atonement, the annual solemn holy day, when the people of Israel would offer an animal sacrifice for the remission of their sins. This act of worship and repentance brought people back into right relationship with God as a fulfillment of the righteous demands of the law. Righteousness in the Hebrew language is the word *tsedeq*, meaning "what is right or just or normal, rightness, justness (of weights and measures)." The Day of Atonement had implications for both personal righteousness (peace between God and God's people) as well as social righteousness (peace between neighbors). This social righteousness parallels what Jesus taught in Matthew 5:23–24: "If you are offering your gift at the altar and there remember that your brother or sister has something against you, leave your gift there in front of the altar. First go and be reconciled to them; then come and offer your gift." Right relationship with God is directly correlated to how people live in right relationship with others, in both word and deed.

Biblical righteousness inherently contains a public quality that is undeniable. Proverbs 29:2 states how "when the righteous are in authority, the people rejoice; but when a wicked man rules, the people groan" (NKJV). The Bible is replete with many examples of the impact the righteous have in political leadership.

Nehemiah was such a leader. As an exile, Nehemiah served as a cupbearer to King Artaxerxes of Persia. In this trusted role, Nehemiah had the trust of the king, and with divine influence he was able to obtain resources from the monarchy to be used toward Jerusalem's redevelopment. Years after the city had been ransacked by Babylon, the walls would be rebuilt and the gates replaced for the well-being and safety of the city's inhabitants. As the people settled into a new era of promise, however, the most vulnerable among them were either being enslaved or losing land to their fellow Israelites.

Echoes of Jubilee are found in Nehemiah chapter 5, as Nehemiah challenges his fellow Israelites around their economic dealings with their kin.

> Now the men and their wives raised a great outcry against their fellow Jews. Some were saying, "We and our sons and daughters are numerous; in order for us to eat and stay alive, we must get grain."

Others were saying, "We are mortgaging our fields, our vineyards and our homes to get grain during the famine."

Still others were saying, "We have had to borrow money to pay the king's tax on our fields and vineyards. Although we are of the same flesh and blood as our fellow Jews and though our children are as good as theirs, yet we have to subject our sons and daughters to slavery. Some of our daughters have already been enslaved, but we are powerless, because our fields and our vineyards belong to others."

When I heard their outcry and these charges, I was very angry. I pondered them in my mind and then accused the nobles and officials. I told them, "You are charging your own people interest!" So I called together a large meeting to deal with them and said: "As far as possible, we have bought back our fellow Jews who were sold to the Gentiles. Now you are selling your own people, only for them to be sold back to us!" They kept quiet, because they could find nothing to say.

So I continued, "What you are doing is not right. Shouldn't you walk in the fear of our God to avoid the reproach of our Gentile enemies? I and my brothers and my men are also lending the people money and grain. But let us stop charging interest! Give back to them immediately their fields, vineyards, olive groves and houses, and also the interest you are charging them—one percent of the money, grain, new wine and olive oil."

"We will give it back," they said. "And we will not demand anything more from them. We will do as you say" (vv. 1–12).

Nehemiah was hearing the cries of the vulnerable of Jerusalem. Weighing heavily was the misery of an economic yoke, stemming from interest on loans they could not repay. Historically it was reminiscent of the cries of the people of Israel in Exodus, as it too was connected to enslavement and the hardships of labor. The image of God was marred as the people of Israel were dehumanized to sustain an Egyptian economy built on slave labor. In Exodus it was the misery and cries of the Hebrew people that rose to heaven, which led God to send a liberator and emissary in Moses.

Centuries later Nehemiah would practice a restitutive form of leadership that challenged the people back to right relationship—particularly around their economic dealings with one another—with slaves being freed, debts being canceled, and the land being restored to owners who had lost it. Notice, the spirit of the conversation between Nehemiah and the people of Israel echoed the ethics of the law of Moses and the mandates of Jubilee.

The people of Yahweh were to steward resources in ways that would affirm their calling as a people to be a light to the nations. By their stewardship of resources and their economic dealings, they were to aspire to be distinct from the surrounding countries. Rebuilding the walls and the gates of Jerusalem was not enough; they were to build a new society within a larger society—one that would be righteous in its dealings within the community. This was Israel's understanding of the law within their storied history. One critique, of course, is that Israel's Jubilee economics was not extended to the gentiles. Thankfully, close to five hundred years later, justice circled back through Jesus's Jubilee (see Interlude: The Jubilee of Jesus), which would be a plan for all people.

Time again in history and Scripture, we see the responsibility for restitution laid on those with privilege and influence as a collective responsibility to act on behalf of societies' most vulnerable. On the other hand, human history has shown that people in power rarely give up resources without a challenge. Abolitionist Frederick Douglass once wrote, "Power concedes nothing without a demand. It never did and it never will."[3] The question is when justice circles back, who will honor its demands for a more just society? One of the hindrances to restitutive justice is when the privileged amass the resources in ways that create significant inequities.

Eco-miseries and Privilege

Jesus witnessed his own people's economic yoke in first-century Rome. According to Dr. Obery Hendricks, quoting N. Sherwin-White,

> The world reflected in the gospels presents "two classes, the very rich and the very poor." The "very rich" in Israel were a tiny upper class, no more than 5 percent of the population. It was composed of Roman bureaucrats, aristocratic priests, a handful of rich landowners, and successful tax collectors. The rest of the people of Israel were poor, many to the point of destitution. . . . Matthew's Gospel tells of standing pools of unemployed village workers so desperate for a day's wages

that they accepted work without even asking how much they would be paid. (Matthew 20:1–16; note vv. 3–7)[4]

Hendricks describes how Jesus contended with economic factors such as poverty, overtaxation, and debt. Being witness to the exploitation of his day, Jesus's parables and metaphors often addressed matters of money, economy, and actual situations related to labor and well-being. Jesus's cleansing of the temple was justice cycling back to a system that had become corrupt, with the priests amassing wealth by taxing the poor.

Today it is difficult to imagine a world where the economic scales are reset, freeing those impacted by poverty from the burdens of debt; providing them with opportunities to have resources to be passed down to younger generations. Instead, income inequality remains part of the normative narrative in the United States. According to incomeequality.org,

> Income disparities are so pronounced that America's top 10 percent now average more than nine times as much income as the bottom 90 percent, according to data analyzed by UC Berkeley economist Emmanuel Saez. Americans in the top 1 percent tower stunningly higher. They average over 39 times more income than the bottom 90 percent. But that gap pales in comparison to the divide between the nation's top 0.1 percent and everyone else. Americans at this lofty level are taking in over 196 times the income of the bottom 90 percent.

Just as we have so-called ghettos of poverty, we can also have ghettos of wealth. Affluence and privilege can keep the church far away from those impacted by the misery of poverty. Professor and prophetic writer Walter Brueggemann writes, "We live our lives out of our affluence, and we discover that all our self-indulgence makes us satiated but neither happy nor safe."[5] Meanwhile the consistent story of Scripture reveals that poverty must be addressed intentionally.

Economic discipleship as part of our Christian formation, can serve to challenge the ways in which Christians live within the arrangements of capitalism—mostly without interrogation. Adam Smith, the father of capitalism, ought not have the final say on the stewardship practices of Christ's followers. Rather, Christians of consciousness can begin to reckon with how in the "inescapable network of mutuality," we are all impacted by poverty and disparity.

The Land Belongs to Whom?

I (José) am not promoting one economic system over another, but rather narrowing the context of this conversation to the church and our spiritual formation. I'm offering an invitation to take a constructive, even critical look at how even our conceptions of ownership can stunt the movement of generosity. God's declaration in Leviticus 25:23, "The land is mine," provides a framework for how Israel was to approach stewardship of the territories beneath the soles of their feet. The land was part of God's jurisdiction of love, a gift to the people, and an extension of God's ecosystem. How does knowing that God is the Creator and Sustainer who entrusts us with resources influence our view of ownership? How could this truth challenge us to reimagine or even expand our notion of ownership? How might it challenge business owners or individuals and institutions that own land?

On a micro level, I often think about the mindset one has when leasing a car rather than owning one. Those who lease might feel a distinct sense of obligation toward care, knowing the car will be returned after a certain amount of mileage and usage. Mindful stewardship would perhaps have us revisit who gets to use the car, borrow it, or even share in its ownership. Perhaps the stakes are different knowing the car will be returned to the dealership, where one will render account for its condition. What the leasing mindset does is have us reassess our relationship to the car in ways that can be more accountable. In essence, stewardship can influence our relationship to the concept of ownership as American.

Reframing Ownership

How do we followers of Jesus, on a micro, mezzo, and macro level, reimagine ownership more expansively? How do we free the land for the people in a world where land consistently becomes commodified—in a culture where private property is part of the normative way to make economic gains? Perhaps wrestling with these questions will fill us with tension, even disorientation; those in churches who hold excessive amounts of property will have to consider more creative ways of engaging "their stuff."

One place we can begin is to trace back to where our distorted notions of land ownership derived. Dr. Willie Jennings notes,

When early Europeans explored the rest of the world, they decided they had "come into possession" of the land. They adopted a particular idea about the land: The land was something that could be "owned" by individuals forever. The strangeness and absurdity of this notion—that the earth can be owned—got lost, and we got accustomed to looking at the earth as a thing. Then Christians rebaptized this view by saying God gave us dominion over the planet, the right to exploit it, extract from it. This has made us oblivious to a sense of place and landscape. We talk about the earth in the language of possession, property, real estate, price point, borders, the boundaries of my land versus yours.[6]

The first place we can begin is evaluating our language around possessions and property. A Jubilee ethics can disrupt the language and logics Christians have about land and place. Good stewardship perhaps begins with better questions, even language about the use of land and space. Jennings points out that our approach to land usually results in three typical questions: (1) "Who owns it?" (2) "How do I extract from it what I need?" and (3) "What piece of land should I possess—that is, where's the best place I can live?"[7]

Part of the engagement Jennings recommends for the church is participation and ownership in local decision-making processes about the use of land. For one, Christians with a Jubilee mindset can see the neighborhoods as a commons. "The commons are the things that we inherit and create jointly, and that will (hopefully) last for generations to come. The commons consists of gifts of nature such as air, oceans and wildlife as well as shared social creations such as libraries, public spaces, scientific research and creative works."[8]

By participating in processes that determine how neighborhoods are organized or rezoned, we can more clearly assess the needs in our neighborhood. A rezoning is where the city government (often with local community input) designates how land and space are used in a community. I had the opportunity to be a part of this process as a resident and church pastor in East Harlem a few years ago.

Ownership in the Neighborhood Planning Processes

East Harlem, originally inhabited by the Munsee Lenape tribe, is one of the areas in Greater Harlem most impacted by poverty. For years now it has also been gentrifying. Walking through the neighborhood, one can see the many telltale signs, such as the scaffolding surrounding future multimillion-dollar brownstones. Permits posted on the green plywood that typically corrals construction sites advertising that "luxury condominiums" are coming soon.

In 2015 New York mayor Bill DeBlasio implemented the city's plan to construct more than two hundred thousand units of affordable housing. East Harlem was one of five neighborhoods that would be rezoned as part of this effort. At the rezoning meeting, the community could get educated on some of the complicated jargon of a rezoning process. It was there I learned about Area Median Income (AMI) and how AMIs determined what was defined as affordable housing. The problem with how AMI was calculated was due the geographic boundaries used in the formula. The calculations included a broad geographic area stretching to include more higher income neighborhoods located miles from Harlem. The question then of what affordability means in more poverty impacted areas becomes less clear.

Other concerns like how high a building development should rise considering surrounding structures came into question. For some, it was a matter of preserving the architectural integrity of a neighborhood with only a few high-rises in proportion to lower-standing buildings. My time spent with different constituents in the neighborhood came with a lot of politics, conflict, and distrust around housing and the use of space. While these conversations were often arduous, it was a conversation the church needed to participate in to ensure that the process had the needs of the most vulnerable in mind.

This level of engagement, even with just one or two dedicated people from our churches, can be a practice of faithful presence. Churches can even learn how their neighbors in the beloved community are managing the dynamics of gentrification. More deeply, though, is the matter of how a community can take ownership of a rezoning process even in the midst of an imperfect process. Churches can also help amplify the voices of other activists who have been doing this kind of neighborhood work for much longer, and whose interests are aligned with shalom. In a big city, the church does not often wield the most influence at every political table, but it can prayerfully participate. And prayer does make a difference.

In Jeremiah 29 the prophet, challenging the exiles, encouraged them to seek the shalom of Babylon, in part by praying for its peace and prosperity. When the church participates in community board processes, the church can encourage church members, in partnership with other churches, to pray specifically around agendas, policies, new businesses, and new visions. Prayer walks and prayer agendas can be formed in ways that imagine a common flourishing in a neighborhood with others. Pastors can also organize and curate neighborhood prayer walks; local pilgrimages can result in new knowledge about the neighborhood's past, present, and future.

Churches may believe they have little influence over neighborhood decision-making, but participation, partnership and informed prayer are powerful means of engagement. Jubilee thinking is an opportunity for the church to contribute to the reimagining and repurposing of place for the benefit of others, especially those who are disinherited through gentrification. If we pray for God's will to be done on earth as it is in heaven, Heaven can emerge as a just partner.

While the church can have direct and indirect impacts on the use of land in neighborhoods, in other contexts there are more direct possibilities. Especially when churches own land, and even have the power to return it to its original inhabitants.

Churches and the #LandBack Movement

The #LandBack movement was formed in 2018 by Aaron Tailfeathers, a member of the Kainai Tribe of Canada. This movement focuses on the reclamation of lands lost due to settler colonialism and reimagines the return of the land for the purposes of preservation, as well as the teaching of indigenous ways when it comes to the care of the land. Therefore, the church's participation is potentially critical in this endeavor, as Christian history has been mired by a theology that justified removing the original inhabitants from their lands.

Through the Doctrine of Discovery in 1452, justified by the papal bull of Romanus Pontifix, non-Christians in other territories were declared enemies of the church. European Christians used the doctrine as the primary justifier for the usurping of territories in the Americas. Hence, European Christians saw themselves as entitled and chosen to take these lands and convert their people. Mark Charles, speaker, writer, and member of the Navajo Tribe writes,

> It feels like our indigenous peoples are an old grandmother who lives in a very large house. It is a beautiful house with plenty of rooms and comfortable furniture. But years ago, some people came into her house and locked her upstairs in the bedroom. Today her home is full of people. They are sitting on her furniture. They are eating her food. They are having a party in her house. They have since come upstairs and unlocked the door to her bedroom, but now it is much later, and she is tired, old, weak and sick; so she can't or doesn't want to come out. But what is the most hurtful and what causes her the most pain, is that virtually no one from this party ever comes upstairs to find the grandmother in the bedroom. No one sits down next to her on the bed, takes

her hand, and simply says, "Thank you. Thank you for letting us be in your house."[9]

Charles's statement calls the church beyond a momentary pause for repentance, but a continual contemplation about the ways Native tribes have been harmed and made invisible. It is reminiscent of Jesus's word in Matthew 25 and how he is vicariously manifested in the most vulnerable (i.e., strangers, imprisoned, thirsty, those without clothes), with Jesus in this case as the Native grandmother who offers a house with many rooms that were taken by force.

Churches are beginning to participate in acts of repentance by integrating this conversation into the liturgical sphere. I've witnessed churches and denominations leading land acknowledgements at the beginning of events or church services, recognizing the places they inhabit as once being the sacred lands of specific Native tribes.

While some churches and denominations have made formal statements repudiating the Doctrine of Discovery, some denominations are also participating in a macro-level effort to return land back to Native tribes. George Tinker, an Osage scholar, describes the efforts saying, "Churches just get to be first in line to show the political system the will and the means for doing it. . . . Name one congregation in the United States that is not located on Indian land."[10]

In 2019 United Methodist Global Missions participated in a Jubilee effort, giving back three acres of ancestral land to the Wyandotte Nation located in Upper Sandusky, Ohio. The Wyandotte Mission was one of forty-nine United Methodist

Heritage Landmarks. This story was no ordinary story of land being stolen away from a Native American tribe. Rather, there was a long-standing relationship between the United Methodist Church and the Wyandotte Nation.

John Steward, the son of enslaved parents, was the UMC's first missionary to this territory. He befriended the Wyandotte tribe and established the UMC's first mission on Wyandotte land. Goodwill was established in a way that bonded the Wyandotte and the UMC for generations to come. The fruit of this bond was demonstrated further when the Wyandotte Nation deeded the UMC with the land for 176 years—to be protected and returned because of the threat of the Indian Removal Act of 1830. Over a century later, the UMC council made good on a generational promise to return the land. This was no mere transaction, as the UMC had been cultivating friendship with the Wyandotte Nation. In honor of the friendship, the Wyandotte Nation will preserve the church located on its land, and the land will be seen as a collective heritage. Somehow, out of a deep history surrounded by the forces of settler colonization, came a unique expression of community and partnership for the present day. The stewardship of the land changed hands in a way that honored the land as sacred.

Members of the UMC and the Wyandotte Nation even participated in a ceremony as a time for celebration and rejoicing titled "A Remembrance of Our Shared History: The Wyandotte/Wyandot and the People Called Methodists."[11] Justice circled back in the honoring of a promise, recognizing the tribe's and the UMC's imperfect yet inextricable history together in all its complexity. What brought them together was displacement and injustice, but the bond of community and a just mindset made way for restitution.

Jubilee for Just Labor

Labor was intended by God to be good but instead has fallen captive to the exploitative nature of our labor market. Meanwhile, labor arrangements can also contribute to the daily lived misery of those in the workforce. Every day, people can wake up feeling inspired or dreadful about their work day; they can return home feeling defeated, stressed, or ill from toxic work cultures.

At the extreme, there are corrupt forms of labor that exploit human beings, even within our own neighborhoods. Consider exploitative labor practices like human sex trafficking in which people take ownership of human resources, using human bodies for profit. Thankfully there are faith organizations advocating against and raising awareness about human sex trafficking, providing an exodus for many who have been enslaved.

Organizations such as Restore NYC work to educate churches and the larger society about human enslavement and sex trafficking. Part of their mission is to facilitate freedom and well-being for survivors of sex trafficking in the form of economic empowerment and housing. According to the data, 94 percent of victims of human sex trafficking are women, with 64 percent of these being Black and Latino.[12]

Restore describes a case like Carmen, who was drawn by her boyfriend, Carlos, from Honduras, on the promise of a better life. When she arrived at the workplace, the job promised to her did not exist. Instead, she was forced into sex labor at a massage parlor. Parlors like these tend to be prevalent in big cities like New York, where underground networks can more easily be formed. Over time Carmen was able to escape, finding Restore NYC, who provided her with a job and the resources she needed to start a new life. When COVID-19 happened, she lost her job at the restaurant where she was working. Yet Restore NYC was able to provide money for her to cover her basic needs. Restore's mission is also attuned to the conditions that can conspire to spawn exploitative labor. Restore reports that neighborhoods most vulnerable to trafficking are the ones most impacted by classicism and racism. Many of the victims and survivors live in low-income neighborhoods, placing the church close to this matter.

Local churches can participate in ministries to those who are trafficked. For ten years our church has supported an organization called Pathfinders, which advocates against human sex trafficking in both New York City and Nigeria. Evon Idahosa is the founding executive director and has been a longtime member of our church. Our church was instrumental in providing Pathfinders with seed money to do this very important work. Churches may find members like Evon looking to live out their ministry calling outside of the traditional means. Through seeding and supporting these calls to ministry, churches can become early adopters and close partners in the liberation of women all over the world.[13]

Stewarding the Labor Force

We all, through our work, can contribute to culture, creativity, and the well-being of others. Every person created in God's image ought to have this sacred gift and opportunity. Jubilee ethics can thus be tied to individual, collective, and even institutional well-being. Any labor performed, and its fruit, can be seen as contributing to the esteem, dignity, and flourishing of human beings in work environments. Since people spend significant time and energy in the workplace, work cultures can become environments where the dignity that derives from being God's image bearer can be affirmed across industries.

How is "good news" made manifest for the person who is exploited for the profit their labor can produce? If "on earth as it is in heaven" means heaven has broken into our reality, how are labor practices honoring the image of God in people in their nine-to-five or nine-to-nine jobs?

People in charge of labor, in all its forms, can recognize the power they hold to either support individual and collective well-being or create conditions that reinforce toxic stress. They can either cultivate conditions that reinforce an insatiable capitalist ethic or cultivate cultures that foster the right relationship to work.

Jubilee ethics can also free people from exploitative labor in an overworked society. We recognize that the workplace is an ecosystem where our labor and its flourishing are bound up with the labor and flourishing of others. Jubilee cannot be just for some while others experience an exploitative labor market.

Business owners and stewards of organizations wield much power and influence on the daily lived experiences of employees when it comes to stress and overwork. According to Fairleigh Dickinson University, "Workplace stress costs U.S. employers an estimated $200 billion per year in absenteeism, lower productivity, staff turnover, workers' compensation, medical insurance and other stress-related expenses. Considering this, stress management may be business's most important challenge of the 21st century."[14]

Many prayer requests go up in churches every week around oppressive work cultures. These range from Fortune 500 companies to small nonprofits, to the local bodegas. Addressing the epidemic of stress happening in the workplace means stewarding the ecosystems connected to policies. These policies can provide benefits and workplace rhythms contributing to employee satisfaction.

One entrepreneur, Jeff Davidson, put his faith into work when he founded a company called Camp Gladiators, a fast-growing fitness company. Davidson does not just champion customer satisfaction but cares for his employees as well—so much so that he integrates his faith into human resources policies. This is an often-overlooked dimension of both nonprofits and for-profit enterprises. Much of the business emphasis can often be placed on customer service and satisfaction, at the cost of the very staff who serve the customers. As part of espousing an abundance approach, Davidson gives his Camp Gladiator employees unlimited time off. He has confidence and trust that well-rested employees will perform well and will also want to return to the work they love. Camp Gladiator is also working to improve their maternity leave policies. Adopting generous labor policies such as these can foster liberative spaces where people are valued and feel a sense of care

Purifying Our Approaches

Jubilee was an ancient law, narrowly observed by the people of Israel yet undeniable in its ethical wisdom toward shaping a form of economic discipleship today. Jubilee as a practice can help us reassess our approaches to land and the stewardship within a workforce ecosystem.

Discerning the ethics of Jubilee also holds robust possibilities for restoring and purifying the imbalances and injustices of wealth on micro, mezzo, and macro levels. For Israel the law was reflected in the restorative measures concerning land, labor, and debt release as part of the Sabbath cycle. Jubilee, then, was good news for those on the "underside" of Israel's economic dealings.

Followers of Christ who hold the privilege of owning businesses, or hold influence in the workplace, like Nehemiah, have an opportunity to create cultures and practices of liberation, as a counterculture to overwork, stress, and anxiety. Elements of Sabbath and Jubilee can even be integrated into workplace policies to encourage health and wellness as a priority.

The gravitational pull of unfettered capitalism will continue to require the liberating Jubilee justice of Christ. The church's formative task then is to join the momentum of a justice that circles back to make things right.

THE JUBILEE OF JESUS: OUR MANIFESTO

In 2008, Disney's Marvel launched a twenty-three-movie mega series, called the Infinity Saga. The Infinity wars would culminate after more than a decade, with multiple heroes teaming up against an alien Titan named Thanos. Thanos's tireless quest was to obtain six gems for the Infinity Gauntlet, which allowed him to wield ultimate power to reimagine and remake the universe in his image. Thanos's crusades brought the good news of Thanos to each galaxy in his quest. With each destination, Thanos would send his forerunner and emissary, Ebony Maw, who would declare these gospel words: "Hear me and rejoice! You have had the privilege of being saved by the Great Titan. You may think this is suffering. No . . . it is salvation. The universal scales tip toward balance because of your sacrifice. Smile . . . for even in death, you have become children of Thanos."

Thanos's economic plan was simple: reduce 50 percent of the universe's population, with this austerity measure ensuring everyone would have enough resources to live. Once this plan was put in place, Thanos could then sit back and observe a "grateful universe," living in a place of abundance because of his magnanimity. Instead, what he found was an ungrateful universe attempting to thwart his quest; Earth's mightiest heroes would craftily retrieve the gauntlet and undo Thanos's handiwork.

Whether in fiction or in real life, empires over time have announced their plans for the world and have exercised their "holy" imaginations. They have imposed their wills on ecosystems, acting as invasive species and have taken over land, people, bodies, culture, and politics to create a world in their image: "on earth as it is in heaven."

In modern-day democracies, politicians use their political platforms to paint a picture of the world in an attempt to arouse the imaginations of potential voters. Political platforms present a candidate's priorities and plans for determining where vital resources will be invested for the good of the people. They can also provide a window into the candidate's imagination about the world to come if their plans were adopted and were set in motion.

Jesus's visit to his hometown of Galilee in some ways is the announcement of a political platform.[1] His Jubilee announcement was for the people from his hometown village, which history suggests boasted a population of somewhere around two hundred. Jesus went to the synagogue and opened the scroll of the book of Isaiah, and read,

> "The Spirit of the Lord is on me,
>> because he has anointed me
>> to proclaim good news to the poor.
> He has sent me to proclaim freedom for the
>> prisoners
>> and recovery of sight for the blind,
> to set the oppressed free,
>> to proclaim the year of the Lord's favor."
>
> Then he rolled up the scroll, gave it back to the attendant and sat down. The eyes of everyone in the synagogue were fastened on him. He began by saying to them, "Today this scripture is fulfilled in your hearing." (Luke 4:18–21)

Nazareth held questionable influence for such an important announcement. What is more, those in attendance at the rally did not know it was a rally. Scripture relates how people in the synagogue were impressed with Rabbi Jesus's reading. According to Shane Claiborne and Chris Haw, "If we might call Jesus president, we could say his campaign slogan was 'Jubilee!' Just like Isaiah had done many years before, Jesus called upon the great economic tradition of the Torah, the counter imperial way of life."[2]

Something went awry, however, when Jesus claimed to be extending his plan for Jubilee to the gentiles. Jesus's plan would reference the story of a poverty-stricken gentile, a widow of Zarephath, who gave the last provisions of her household to the prophet Elijah. And in faith, her bread provided not only for the prophet but for her household. God's hands had worked through her hands; Jesus's reference would cast the enemies of Israel as participants in God's miracles. This moment also ran counter to the conventional teachings they had historically received, namely, in seeing the gentiles as outsiders to God's covenant with Israel.

Imagining a Crossover

Jesus was ushering forth a kingdom shalom, a form of peace operating in stark contrast to *Pax Romana*, the peace and good news of Rome. Rome's good news was a form of peace largely established by force and one that would ensure the stability of an economy for the ruling elites. In contrast, Jesus's peace would bring forth good news to the poor, an unprecedented form of reaching "across the aisle" even to those considered the enemy. The social arrangements that Israel had embraced for centuries were now being disturbed. For the Jews, their ways of being in the world, even their contempt for the gentiles would be challenged. And the fact that Jesus, in his own village of Nazareth, would audaciously elevate the oppressors into three-dimensional human form, was the ultimate disruption, a disruption punishable by being shoved over the brow of a Nazarene cliff.

Jesus was conjuring two memories for the people. Israel, for one, had a history of ridding themselves of truth tellers, namely, the prophets. And by referencing the widow of Zarephath, he was demonstrating that signs of covenant had always been extended to the gentiles. Yet Jesus was also appealing to their collective vocation as a people. For the name

Hebrew itself literally means "a people who cross over"—who transgress boundaries through the leading of the Holy Spirit.

Crossing over into Jubilee-way would also be an initiation into the body of Christ, a bridging moment revealed to the apostle Paul, who wrote in Galatians 3:28, "There is neither Jew nor Gentile, neither slave nor free . . . you are all one in Christ Jesus." Out of the many messiahs who appeared in the first century, there was no messianic precedent for what Jesus ushered forth in this form of crossover. Jesus was going to diversify the ecosystem through his reign. Jesus's Jubilee logic would reach across ethnic and class lines and apply to rich and poor alike; it would be transgressive in its challenge to people to cross all social strata in this vision of the kingdom. Why?

Because God so loved the world.

Only God can hold the whole of this vision for the entire world. So how does something so grand translate into the micro worlds we know as neighborhoods? If we thought of it in such terms, this dream would remain abstract, disembodied even from a place, severed from the imaginations of the church. What humble role can the church play in this great Jubilee enterprise? Tim Soerens, author and cofounder of Parish Collective, helps us find our footing:

> If we hope to engage God's healing dream, we need an approach that simultaneously honors individual people, the systems we have created, the dynamic relationship in which people influence systems, and systems influence people. By naming the parish as the unit of change, we reclaim the parish as the literal ground where practiced faith becomes a

powerful and even subversive organizing platform. The parish gives shape and definition to our imagination as we dream about real people and real places and their very real stories. . . . If we dare to imagine what God's dream might be, and we want to follow the Spirit, then we need a shared geography to move us from an abstract idea to a very real dream. The parish is the playground where God can invite us into practical hope.[3]

Parish is an ancient word and another way of describing a church's geographic area of care. The opportunity for the church is its participation in God's healing vision for people and places. Jesus's Jubilee platform through the Spirit inspires and animates new possibilities for bringing street-level hope. Prayerfully, this will begin with, as they say in politics, "working across the aisle" to engage the social fragmentation that keeps needing mending. Fragmentation comes in many forms, but the good news is that we have been liberated into divine initiative. For any time the church digs new ground across class, race, gender, or geographic divides in pursuit of renewal, it is reflective of Jesus's Jubilee platform. Who wouldn't want to endorse a platform with a Spirit of love as its animating force?

Loving and Inviting Wealth Holders

Jesus said the love of money is the root of evil. For Americans with wealth, Jesus's words ought to create a healthy, even nagging tension—namely, that money does indeed have the power to change hearts and dispositions, even in subtle ways. One probably can't know how much they love money until challenged to give up some of its luxuries. Money can also distance people from the impacts of poverty and, by default, distance them from *the people* directly impacted by poverty. The distance for crossing over to join those in need can become an ever-widening gap. But the church is called to shorten the distance through inviting the rich and wealthy.

Ron Sider wrote,

> Most . . . Christians have failed to seek God's perspective on the plight of our billion plus desperately poor neighbors—surely one of the most pressing issues of our time. But I refuse to believe that this failure must inevitably continue. I believe there are millions of affluent Christians who are more about Jesus than anything else in the world. There are millions of Christians who will take any risk, make any sacrifice, forsake any treasure, if they see clearly that God's word demands it.[4]

Sider was recognizing the need to engage wealthy Christians, spread in neighborhoods across the world, who can make a just impact in a world impacted by poverty. Jesus once attempted to enlist a young rich ruler. In Mark 10:17–31, Mark told the story of a rich man who approached Jesus and asked, "What must I do to inherit eternal life?" In this encounter, there's a subtle portion of the text people often overlook. In people's earnest reading of the text, they will leap into Jesus's challenge to sell everything he has and give to the poor. Overlooked is the portion of Scripture that first says, "Jesus looked at him and loved him." Jesus's prophetic challenge to the rich young ruler was first initiated through love. Jesus knew well how this man needed his own Jubilee from the prison of wealth. He found himself on the other side of the Jubilee cycle, where his identity was wrapped up in his possessions.

This statement demonstrates Jesus's approach to those with privilege. It would be far easier to *exclusively* focus on potentially ill-gotten gains. Some scholars speculate that the rich man might have accumulated wealth from the all-too-common practice of confiscating land from those unable to pay their debts, capitalizing on the misfortune of others. Yet Jesus did not create a caricature out of this man as the young rich ruler found himself facing questions that dealt with life and death. Jesus's attempt to lead him to the path of eternal life meant transgressing the class boundaries that distanced the wealthy from the poor. Jesus challenged the man's present social arrangement. What is more, the rich man, in surrendering his possessions, *could have* served as an agent of Jubilee for others who may have received restitution from his wealth, not unlike the Zacchaeus, the tax collector who upon meeting Jesus committed to giving back four times what he stole from his fellow Israelites (Luke 19:8).

The apostle Paul enlisted the support of a European business woman named Lydia (Acts 16) to support the work of establishing church communities. Alexia Salvatierra describes how the work of Base Ecclesial Communities, the original "micro church" movement of Latin America and the Philippines, enlisted Lydia types, people of privilege to support the liberating work of these small lay-led movements.[5]

Invitations to people of privilege can serve to guide them into distinct roles that honors the work of people impacted by poverty. Meanwhile crossing class lines in this manner can be just as challenging as crossing over racial lines.

Wealth and privilege can become isolating. In *The Soul of Money*, Lynne Twist describes Mother Teresa's perspective on the privileged: "[Wealth is] like a hamster wheel that we hop onto, get going and forget how to stop. Eventually, the chase for more becomes an addictive exercise, and as with any addiction, it's almost impossible to stop the process when you're in its grip."[6]

Yet the rich young ruler transgressed a boundary to speak with Jesus. At the same time, Jesus saw beyond the rich young ruler's wealth; he recognized how the wealth he owned was an obstruction to living a liberated life. Jesus's invitation was also a "call in," not a "call out." This approach can shape the church's conversation in a "call out" culture, offering the rich man an opportunity to repent and return to beloved community. Some will leave in grief at Jesus's invitation because they are bound to their possessions, but the invitation still stands.

Joining the Jubilee Cycle

Jesus's invitation was not for the rich man to throw away his riches but to gift them to people impacted by poverty. He was to open his hands in a sacrificial way and enter God's economy—a place where the gift would continue to circulate for the blessing of the ecosystem. Entering into God's subversive gift economy is transgressive, as money and resources will bypass the traditional channels to meet the needs. Jubilee also initiates a gift-giving economy in which the rich are no longer separated from people impacted by poverty; the nature of the exchange being the gift of mutuality that comes from being the beloved community.

While the rich man was not ready to join Jesus's Jubilee campaign, as Sider mentioned earlier, there are many Christians with means who are desiring to join Jesus's campaign for the world. Many of us are at the intersections of holding different forms of privilege. For one thing, simply being born in North America places middle-class people in the top tenth percentile when it comes to wealth worldwide. Many of us have the privilege of being liberated to exercise our gifts in this world. By virtue of this, we are given the capacity to do the serious work of healing the divides that fragment our worlds.

We can cross over, seeking to integrate individuals and communities into God's dream for the neighborhood. In part, this means small actions and big imagination. Jesus spoke about the reign of God in start-up metaphors, such as mustard seeds and starter dough. He told stories about the reign of God starting small and expanding. He focused on the aspirational nature of the reign of God, essentially, how the reign of God is already here and not yet. Jesus will continue to invite, while the Spirit will continue to lead.

I (José) would like to campaign, with millions of others, for Jesus's Jubilee invitation during this new season of the church. Following is a platform for the church in towns, cities, suburbs, and rural areas.

A 7-Point Manifesto Inspired by Jesus's Jubilee Platform

1. As the church of Christ, we will pray for our neighborhoods individually and collectively. This will include embodied prayers, "praying with our feet," walking through our neighborhoods with sacred curiosity, even marching together when the time calls for it. We will discern our sacred role as part of the fellowship of the neighborhood. As curators of our local ecosystems, we recognize this prayerful task permeates neighborhood life on the individual, communal, and systemic level.

2. We are committed to God's "harmony way." As the church in the neighborhood, as part of God's small unit of change, we believe mission can be framed around patterns of "faithful presence" and contextual practices, where even just two or three can gather in Christ's name. We join God, one another, and our neighbors in the gospel of liberation, beginning where Jubilee begins: with the most vulnerable in our world.

3. In the Spirit of creation and biodiversity, we believe that on a small scale we can participate in mustard-seed movements, bringing indigenous wisdom, the business community, wisdom keepers, and wealth holders into a community of practice. We will, as a church, participate in dismantling and opposing extractive practices in our community. We will consistently keep in mind Christianity's past allegiance to empire, while maintaining a continued posture of repentance and an eye toward reparations.

4. Justice, like Sabbath and Jubilee, is cyclical. We believe justice circles back for us to revisit systems and structures in our neighborhoods that obstruct the circulation of resources and corrode mutuality and reciprocity. We also believe no one totally rests from their labor until the most vulnerable in society are able to rest from theirs.

5. We believe that even in our capitalist society, that the land belongs to the Creator. As part of our economic discipleship, we will pursue more liberative and imaginative ways of thinking about ownership, stewarding what we are privileged to own, for the benefit of more people in our communities. Across contexts we think about the power of space and place to hold and invite people into belonging together, from parks to sidewalks, homes to trailers, and apartments to gardens, even in the farms that produce nourishment for our bodies.

6. As people are created in the image of their Creator, they have all been given gifts to contribute to their neighborhoods and world. Our liberative spaces will make room for the identification and the use of these gifts. The church can get on God's agenda for people in the world. We will advocate for opportunities, in collaboration, to ensure people are compensated for their labor in ways that are just and preserve the dignity of their work. We will work to remove exploitive labor that destroys the dignity of work and obscures the image of God, reducing bodies to units of labor.

7. We believe it is ideology that sustains economic systems. These systems disciple and shape our everyday

approaches to money and commerce, our daily transactions. As a church, we embark on creating distinct agreements with our money and resources that will render open hands and hearts, stewarding our spending. We also both challenge and invite those with means connected to the market to guard their mutual funds and portfolios from the extractive practices of certain global corporations.

I (José) am always on the lookout for small signs of Jubilee, the big little farms that embody new possibility, those who see the signs and wonders of what could be in our neighborhoods and beyond.

Jesus came to our world and led with a Jubilee platform—a divine initiative that would bring the priorities of Heaven into the world: to liberate the prisoner, to free the oppressed, to declare the year of the Lord's favor. With very little fanfare, these signs and wonders can take root today through the experiments of the church in the world. Every time people experience the freedom that comes with Christ, a positive environmental impact can follow, for true salvation is salvation of body, soul, and ecosystem.

Jesus for president.

PART THREE

ECONOMIC ETHICS IN
THE NEIGHBORHOOD

Thus far we have considered how the ethical triad of gleaning, Sabbath, and Jubilee are meant to resist economic injustices brought on by exclusion, extraction, and exploitation. In part 2, we reflected on specific connections between gleaning and exclusion, Sabbath and extraction, and Jubilee and exploitation. Those three *Es* are enemies of a healthy neighborhood ecosystem, and this framework aims to help us push back on those forces.

In part 3, we turn our attention to considering how we might begin to enact this framework in concrete ways in the neighborhood. Bringing gleaning, Sabbath, and Jubilee closer together, we see ways they inform and shape each other and how, in ways large and small, they all resist the forces of economic injustice. In other words, a robust practice of Sabbath not only will help us resist extraction but will help us resist exclusion and exploitation as well. This is true for all three. To bring these three closer together, part 3 focuses on widening our imagination for the *kind* and *character* of the economic life produced by a serious commitment to gleaning, Sabbath, and Jubilee. So a serious commitment to gleaning helps create an economy of sharing and opportunity. Sabbath ethics nurture an economy of restoration. And Jubilee in practice fosters an economy of celebration and ownership. As we consider each in turn, and the interplay of the three together, we will see ways in which these three contribute to a vibrant and healthy life in the neighborhood.

At the same time, we've been in this work long enough to know that the issue is not as simple as providing transferable models that can be implemented wholesale in different communities. So we offer frameworks, case studies, stories, and ideas here as a way of fostering a deeper "theo-practical" imagination, and we trust that in local neighborhoods around the country, good work is being done to understand the specific challenges, contextual nuances, and community needs so that particular strategies can be discerned and implemented.

SIX

GLEANING: AN ECONOMY OF SHARING AND OPPORTUNITY

One of my (Adam) favorite things about having a garden is finding ways to share the produce from that garden with others. Admittedly, I am not the gardener in the house, but I love trying to be creative with the vegetables and herbs that grow in our backyard. We have many friends who do this too. Some bring their bounty to gatherings to give away, some make salsa and share it over a meal together, and I like to invite folks over for grilled flatbreads sprinkled with fresh basil or oregano—there are so many ways to share. It strikes me that there might be some instinct in us that makes us want to share the abundance of our gardens. That instinct, I'd argue, is what makes the gleaning laws so intuitive and what makes them feel so natural. We are meant to share with each other. We aren't meant to hoard. Anytime we don't share the bounty of our gardens, we can't eat it fast enough, and it just goes bad in the fridge anyway. In a delightful expression of God's abundance, even small gardens can produce more than what one person or family can consume. It's almost as if God is training us to practice gleaning.

Those impulses are what we want to build on as we begin to think about how to apply the theological framework from part 2 in our neighborhoods. Healthy neighborhood ecosystems start to take shape through the applied practices of gleaning. In other words, we cultivate a healthier neighborhood ecosystem when we create a community of sharing and opportunity.

Cultivating Sharing and Opportunity

If, as we've argued already, Luke 4 is evidence of Jesus inaugurating a new era for justice that includes the economic ethics of the Old Testament, then it makes sense that we would find similar evidence of the church in the New Testament enacting practices that reflect those ethics. For us to make the claim that these ethics can—and ought to—guide our lives today, we do well to consider the narrative accounts of the first-century church in Acts. When we do that, we find two compelling, complementary descriptions of the way of life the church enacted in the immediate aftermath of Pentecost and the commissioning of the church to participate in the full mission of Jesus and the kingdom of God.

First, in Acts 2 we find this description of the church's way of life:

They devoted themselves to the apostles' teaching and to fellowship, to the breaking of bread and to prayer. Everyone was filled with awe at the many wonders and signs performed by the apostles. All the believers were together and had everything in common. They sold property and possessions to give to anyone who had need. Every day they continued to meet together in the temple courts. They broke bread in their homes and ate together with glad and sincere hearts, praising God and enjoying the favor of all the people. And the Lord added to their number daily those who were being saved. (vv. 42–47)

The second description is found two chapters later in Luke's account and adds some extra color to fill out our picture of life in the first-century church:

All the believers were one in heart and mind. No one claimed that any of their possessions was their own, but they shared everything they had. With great power the apostles continued to testify to the resurrection of the Lord Jesus. And God's grace was so powerfully at work in them all that there were no needy persons among them. For from time to time those who owned land or houses sold them, brought the money from the sales and put it at the apostles' feet, and it was distributed to anyone who had need.

Joseph, a Levite from Cyprus, whom the apostles called Barnabas (which means "son of encouragement"), sold a field he owned and brought the money and put it at the apostles' feet. (Acts 4:32–37)

The first thing we see when considering these two texts is the relatively comprehensive nature of Luke's description. These accounts show us a wide range of activities and practices of the early church, including their worship and community and public life. This is significant because the economic implications of their life together are inextricably intertwined with their conception of the faithful life of the church and their witness to the lordship of Christ. Willie Jennings notes that in the New Testament church, "matters of money are inescapable. They are at the heart of discipleship."[1] These first-century economic practices are considered radical today. The selling of property and possessions and contributing to a common pool of resources so as to ensure the well-being of the entire community has been argued against or rejected by large streams of Christians. One wonders if this is because these practices challenge the assumptions of capitalism and not orthodoxy because, in the imagination of the first followers of Jesus, these practices seemed incredibly obvious and ordinary. No one had to tell Jesus's first followers to pool their resources; their actions were a natural overflow of the gospel taking root in community. No one was getting clapped on the back for being radical; their giving was, quite simply, the cost of discipleship.

Perhaps even more significant to our discussion of the economic practices of individuals is what those practices signify and produce in the community. In both texts, we see Christians "freeing the edges of their fields" and loosening their grip on the resources in their possession. This is as straightforward an application of an Old Testament ethic in a New Testament context as one might imagine. In doing so, the community is able to flourish. The ecosystem in its entirety thrives because there is no private claim on resources. In God's economy, there is enough for everyone! A flourishing ecosystem of God's community is itself created and sustained through this ongoing practice of gleaning contextualized for the first-century church. Instead of viewing resources as a possession to own, the church sees resources as a well that can sustain everyone. In other words, the community that practices gleaning in context is nurturing a *sharing economy* in ways that open up opportunity for everyone to flourish.[2]

A Sharing Economy

A sharing economy is an economy of the open hand in lieu of the culturally accepted notion of an economy of privatized, competitive ownership. The sharing economy helps to produce the harmony envisioned by God in the first place. Gleaning challenges us to resist accepting credit for philanthropy, as though opening our hands ought to be accompanied by trumpet blasts. Instead, the open hand of gleaning is a response to the God who is doing the work of creating the ecosystem that can flourish. We are not to get the credit; we are collaborators in a work of liberation and new life.

One could point to Luke's naming of Joseph at the end of Acts 4 and argue that even in the text someone is being congratulated for his generosity, though that assumption is challenged as we continue to read Luke's account. Immediately after naming Joseph and his openhanded action, we encounter the account of Ananias and Sapphira in Acts 5, who—together, and in full knowledge of their deception—attempted to fake an openhanded action while firmly maintaining their closed fist on their margin. The disciples' shock at this scandal was magnified because they acknowledged the relative discretion Ananias and Sapphira had over their margin. This is probably an indication that Luke's mention of the early believers having all possessions in common was descriptive more than prescriptive. Ananias and Sapphira were not breaking the law in keeping some of the money but were feigning an open hand while still maintaining control over their finances, which made a mockery of the community's commitment to shared flourishing. This was such a serious offense that we witness the only instance in the New Testament of what looks like God striking someone dead in judgment. Without pretending to know what to make of that, we highlight the serious nature of fidelity to God and the economic implications that accompany it.

Common ownership of the pool of resources was the church's alternative to the system of private ownership all around them. Holding resources in common functioned similarly to the way gleaning provided the poor with access to economic life in community. The common pool was a response to the question of the poor's access to the economic system of the day. They were excluded from the economic system of the status quo, so the church enacted an example of what I once heard urban ministry practitioner Bob Lupton call an "alternative system of exchange." This alternative system of exchange was an economy of sharing.

Rather than try to make a specific argument that the concrete actions from Acts 2 and 4 should be applied to every context today, the common pool of resources can be creatively adapted when we understand it as the creation of an alternative system of exchange that nurtures a sharing economy. When we begin to look at our neighbors and ask, Who gets left out (who doesn't have access) and why? we can start to envision creative systems that nurture a sharing economy as a means of creating access and opportunity for all. Gleaning points us to consider the question of access broadly: Are we creating a community where everyone gets to play? Ecosystems begin to thrive when they start making resources available to the entire community.

To start, this might look something like a community-based benevolence fund, adapting a practice Christians have long engaged in the church, and applying it to the community. Ministers Richard Allen and Absalom Jones created the Free African Society in 1787 with the goal of having funds that could help the poor.[3] That concern for the financial stability of the community has been a hallmark of the Black church in the United States throughout its history, and that approach has been adapted and reimagined in many ways.

In my (Adam's) community, faith groups are managing funds that neighbors give and take from as they have opportunity or need—not a formal loan program but neighbors sharing with one another. Others are working ecumenically to create pools of resources/assets to respond to crisis moments like a sudden influx of refugees. Of course, sharing in times of crisis has long shaped the practices of faith communities and neighborhoods. The question is, how might we extend the sharing ethos that arises during a crisis to ordinary life in a community so that neighbors and neighborhoods build resilience and can begin to flourish together?

Carrying Money for Connection

Carrying cash on purpose can lead to moments of connection with people in our neighborhoods. This is a practice I (José) mindfully began a few years ago because money is typically used for specific types of transactions—purchasing goods or services. But having cash on hand can also facilitate a different form of transaction—a human connection.

Cash once helped me connect with a neighbor from a nearby veterans' facility. My son and I were taking a walk to the neighborhood Subway shop, one of his favorite places for cookies. As we approached the entrance, a man sitting nearby asked me for money. We learned that his name was Chuck, and he easily could have been mistaken for someone experiencing homelessness. He appeared disheveled, and his clothing was dirty and oversized. I could've made many assumptions, but I chose curiosity instead.

Chuck told us he lived just down the block at a veterans' facility. As he described his disability, I registered the bigger picture of his situation, like the limited benefits he received as a veteran in New York City, leaving him income insecure. Many veterans like Chuck can be mistaken for people experiencing homelessness. Some have substance use issues, and others need extra income to subsist in Manhattan. Like many large cities, the cost of living in New York City makes the desperate even more so.

Some days I would give Chuck cash or just invite him inside to get something to eat. I realize fully that the lunch I bought with "spare" money may or may not have made his daily reality much easier. Yet these moments create micro connections that otherwise would not have existed. In fact, Chuck could have simply remained another anonymous "panhandler" in my mind, with me just another passerby affirming his invisibility in our big city. Noticing Chuck and "freeing the margins of my money" was one small way I could connect with Chuck . . . and with Christ.

Just as money can mediate connections with strangers in need, so can public spaces. Shared spaces like sidewalks can provide opportunities for care in nontraditional ways. Public spaces can mediate opportunities for sharing in ways that operate outside of the traditional systems of care.

An Open-Fridge Policy

Community refrigerators throughout New York City are beginning to serve an especially important role for those experiencing food insecurities. Community refrigerators are stocked with food for anyone to glean from—no questions asked. Leading one of these initiatives is Bushwick Abbey, a local church in Brooklyn. Bushwick Abbey has partnered with a local organizing hub named May Day to establish a community refrigerator for the neighborhood. Fresh produce and other food items are made available in a neighborhood struggling with food insecurity exacerbated by the COVID-19 pandemic. An "open" refrigerator also communicates hospitality, removing the stigma, while normalizing the needs of those who are benefiting from it.

Bushwick Abbey proudly put up a sign on the refrigerator door that reads: "Take what you need, leave what you can."

The placement of encouraging signs is a form of hospitality and connection created in community, not unlike household refrigerators where families post good grades, art, and family pictures.

What makes these neighborhood connections even more far-reaching is when local businesses participate in the community refrigerator movement. Local restaurants in Harlem participate by providing prepped meals to be placed in community refrigerators. These efforts also form an ecosystem between small businesses and local residents on the block, ensuring people don't go home hungry. When small businesses participate this way, it also expands their mission beyond the scope of profit-making.

The community refrigerator movement harkens back to a long tradition in Black and brown neighborhoods, addressing food insecurities outside the formal channels. While much food goes to waste in our city due to overconsumption, community refrigerators offer food resources from which people can glean.

Open Streets: Freeing Commodified Spaces

Public space is a commodity in many neighborhoods in the US. In places like the suburbs, development tends to favor commercial space and private residential neighborhoods. Hence, being able to close down a block to traffic for the public can be priceless.

The Open Streets initiative is a nationwide movement to reimagine street life for the common good. Local government, nonprofits, or private enterprises can close down street blocks for the purposes of creating community connections. Local neighborhood space is reimagined and reconfigured to accommodate healthy activities like yoga, biking, or basketball, or even promoting local businesses that can set up pop-up shops. Open Streets is different from organizing, say, a street festival, which is more of a one-off event; it is a street closure sustained over a period of time. Churches can see this as a sustained opportunity to collaborate with other agencies around repurposing space in neighborhoods, whether in towns, the country, or cities. Broadway Baptist Church was listed as one major contributor to Open Streets in Dallas–Fort Worth, recognizing the value of neighborhood life in partnership with other institutions.

Near me, one neighborhood block association, Marcus Meets Malcolm, was able to close off a block, providing a safe place for children to play. What's more, the space wasn't just intended for their own children; they shared recreational equipment, like a portable basketball hoop with children from neighboring blocks. Marcus Meets Malcom freed up the block from typical traffic to create a whole new social and economic story within the neighborhood.

Open Streets is a positive disruption in a come-and-go city like NYC "Freeing up" the block can form an ecosystem that reorients the rhythms of engagement on the block, with people more apt to stop and have conversations. These counter cultural approaches to life on the block also require area homeowners to be willing to reimagine a stranger's presence into one of a potential neighbor.

Like block associations, what if churches began to think

more creatively about the role of church sidewalks and streets? Churches could potentially create a commons by reimagining space; sidewalks could be transformed into porches where shared space, culture, life, and belonging transform the use of church property.

Discipling through Dollar Chains

Michelle Cruz is an East Harlemite and alumni of Metro Hope Church who has a passion for helping residents of East Harlem spend their money in their own neighborhood. Of the $3 billion spent annually by East Harlem residents on goods and services, $805 million of it is spent outside East Harlem. Through an initiative named Buy Local, Cruz developed relationships between vendors and small businesses and brokered deals that encouraged businesses to buy from local vendors. She also helped execute transactions between the businesses themselves, creating a chain of local dollars that could circulate within East Harlem.

Contemplating dollar chains has been used as a discipleship tool in our church. We describe how one can witness a form of economic shalom by tracking a trail of dollars intentionally spent in the neighborhood. The following is a short chain of documented transactions in our local context:

1. Brenda, a local East Harlem resident, purchases her coffee from Uptown Coffee Beans.
2. Because of regular customers like Brenda, Uptown Coffee Beans is able to hire Maribelle, a local resident, as a server and barista.

3. Maribelle is now able to sign up her daughter for the local soccer team and pay for a uniform through a local business owner, Steve Matias of JC1 Graphx. Steve is then able to hire a local digital marketing consultant called Think Big Data to increase his visibility and online presence.

Tracing the path of resources this way, one can witness how a shared economy is connected to people's livelihood and can encourage shopping local. Exchanges such as this require not only an open hand but the daily discipline and practice of keeping resources circulating through the community in the spirit of gleaning. There is power in an ecosystem of businesses and residents operating from a daily ethos of mutuality.

When Churches Cancel Debts

During the height of the COVID pandemic, many churches were able to provide generous support to those with medical debt. One church in particular, Trinity Church, raised $38,000 to cancel medical debt for expenses that health insurance did not cover for people in the community. Rev. Otis Moss, senior pastor at Trinity United Congregational Church in Chicago said, "Instead of allowing debt collectors to purchase the debt, why not have communities of faith purchase that debt and forgive that debt?" Trinity is one among a number of churches and denominations working to selflessly recirculate church resources for the common good.

Pathway Church in Wichita, Kansas, decided to forgo

spending $22,000 of its budget on its Easter promotion and used it to cancel $25 million in debt. This was made possible by RIP Medical Debt, a company founded by two former debt collectors.[4] RIP buys medical debt at extremely cheaper amounts, providing opportunities for the church to participate and make an impact. RIP has described churches as becoming one of the largest donors to this initiative.

Relieving people from debt can provide income to use at their own discretion. It may make the difference between having to make decisions to pay certain bills as opposed to others, which is not uncommon among those who face economic insecurities daily. There are yet other ways people of faith can free the obstructed circulation of resources and place them back in the hands of the people. Debt relief can also free up discretionary income; it may make the difference between people having to choose between one bill over another (i.e., rent versus food), which is not uncommon. When the church frees up funds to share with others (gleaning), the funds are applied to debt release (Sabbath and Jubilee). Bringing the parts together in one strategy enhances the opportunity and possibility to help a community flourish.

These examples give us ways to imagine all manner of tactics for enhanced sharing of resources and assets, and to draw from experiments in alternative systems of economic inclusion around the nation. Ideas like these are popping up all over the country. In Appalachia, people are creating tool libraries, enabling the entire community to use the tools they need to maintain, repair, and steward properties and land. In cities across the nation, local business groups are creating innovative local systems designed to stimulate support for, and circulate capital among, local business ventures. Inspired by the work of Bob Lupton and others, groups all over have embraced more cooperative approaches to traditional forms of charity that allow greater participation and enable each member of the community to have an increased degree of agency over their future prospects. Community gardens offer a common bounty of food for neighbors to both contribute and consume. Some churches are creating small-scale entrepreneur funds. Neighbors can pitch ideas, and a seed grant fund helps launch hyperlocal economic experiments envisioned by folks who live on the block together. These are ideas that expand our imagination for work we can do to foster a sharing economy.

Gleaning Creates Opportunity: A Daily Tactical Approach

Gleaning pushes our imagination further than only fostering a sharing economy. It challenges us to conceive of ways that our sharing practices can create economic opportunity for others, particularly the economically vulnerable.

In neighborhood ecosystems where financial insecurities are prevalent, residents often find themselves deliberating between paying rent or paying medical debt. These economic stressors can loom large, causing people to live in a constant state of struggling to survive. Mujerista theologian Ada Maria Isasi-Diaz describes the daily experiences, concerns, and survival tactics of the disinherited (particularly women) as *lo cotidiano*.[5] Daily financial concerns can often be overlooked by government policies. The church, as part of a web of collective support, can participate in the "meantime" approaches to engage daily economic concerns. The church in some cases can participate in "the meantime" approaches to engaging neighborhood needs.

In lieu of this, often taken for granted is how church food pantries and dinner programs become these safety nets engaging the lived daily economic insecurities. Just as importantly, these programs convert churches into public spaces where participants can have conversations with one another, much in the same way as people do at a cookout in the park.

Both structural changes and daily formative tactics for engaging economic insecurity are necessary. And multiple approaches by the Christian community are vital for justice and righteousness to be holistic. We need activists who will look at the larger system of resources, and we need to look at the micro daily practices that will alleviate the shortages of a scarcity economy. Churches are specially positioned to engage everyday economic stressors in a manner not unlike the first church.

Cash Mobs: Focused Shopping

Metro Hope Church, the church I (José) colead, has been able to partner with Buy Local East Harlem to organize cash mobs, a crowdsourcing approach to infusing a local business with cash, which can also serve to promote the business. Cash mobs are a simple concept. The process includes the local church cultivating a connection with a local business owner (often a restaurateur). Business owners are encouraged to show up to church the Sunday prior to the cash mob, where they can share about their dreams for the business and also share some highlights of their menu for the cash-mob event.

Church and community members are encouraged to use cash to support that local business on that specific Sunday after church. They are also encouraged to use cash because it circulates and "digests" in a community over three times longer than credit. Since this endeavor has evolved, Buy Local East Harlem has hired our church's worship band to be the local house band for the restaurant. Usually, small establishments can't afford live music, so this cultivates a lively atmosphere with high-quality music. Meanwhile, the church is sharing its talent capital while ensuring its artists and musicians are compensated. Essentially, this is another way we can trace the dollar chain! On the day of the cash mob, at least three or four churches from the neighborhood can be represented. It is not uncommon for local elected officials or community board members to also participate. One of the greatest encouragements comes when a business owner asks, "Why would the church do this? What's in it for the church?"

At one particular cash mob at El Barristas in East Harlem, Emmanuel, the owner, jubilantly shared with the crowd, "I'm so glad people are back [from the pandemic], because the community is supporting us. We need to support the community back with more events! . . . I'm so excited, I keep looking out, and there are so many people, I feel like I'm back in high school and I'm playing sports again, and you guys are cheering us on."

We then proceeded to say a prayer for Emmanuel, blessing his establishment. Moments such as these go a long way for a tired entrepreneur in our community. As church pastors, we realize that cash-mob events might not directly contribute to church attendance or church growth. Instead, the reward is when churches can recognize that they are playing their part in God's sacred ecosystem, "caught in an inescapable network of mutuality."

Cash mobs create a form of intention through a cash agreement that encourages foot traffic to local businesses, directing disciples of Christ to spend their money tactically. Ultimately this is an act of stewardship that forms people and can shape their thinking into God's gift economy.

Cash mobs are a great way to use freed-up capital for neighbor and neighborhood flourishing. Similarly, I (Adam) was part of a project focused on using traditional forms of charitable giving to increase the impact potential in local communities. We were able to create a fund that allowed churches or nonprofits to create small-scale, community-focused economic initiatives (usually, but not always in the form of social enterprise ventures) that created economic development opportunities for their neighbors (one such story we share in chapter 8). Through this—and similar—work, we were able to help groups launch projects like T-shirt shops working with local teenagers, a barber shop / community space, a racial justice–oriented preschool program, among other things. The particulars of the projects were as diverse as the communities represented. The common thread was that each group was using capital for more than a handout. They were creating opportunities for folks to experience a more flourishing future.

This type of work is compelling to folks who want to free the edges of their fields in creative ways and those who aren't concerned about getting a return on their investment. This usually depends on the traditional nonprofit structure, but the spirit of this model is something that can be reimagined at the local level, potentially in ways that deal even more directly with neighbors and the neighborhood. We highlight a few examples of this as we continue.

Getting Started with Gleaning

The fundamental spirit of the gleaning laws was aimed at helping the wealthy, asset-rich members of society loosen their grip on those resources in a way that would create opportunity for the entire community, particularly the poor and those on the margins. Thus, gleaning pushes us to go beyond charitable giving to sharing resources that create opportunities for folks to fashion their own futures.

As you imagine ways to begin practicing gleaning ethics to cultivate an ecosystem of Jubilee, here are a few first steps to consider.

- Conduct a personal (or community) resource/asset audit. Where are resources that could promote the shared flourishing of the neighborhood being stockpiled, blocked, guarded, or otherwise held at arm's length away from the community?
- Perform a neighborhood-based economic SWOT (strengths, weaknesses, opportunities, threats) analysis. With neighbors and friends, look at your neighborhood through the lens of economic strengths, weaknesses, opportunities, and threats. Understanding the realities

ECONOMIC ETHICS IN THE NEIGHBORHOOD

at work in your community will, for example, point you to places where resources are being blocked and therefore creating a threat to the economic vitality of the more vulnerable folks in the neighborhood. Doing a SWOT analysis can also serve as a generative time of idea sharing and collaboration.

- Consider ways of pooling resources for community flourishing. The New Testament examples and many of the modern-day snapshots we shared took on new life and possibility because the people involved worked to gather their resources in common spaces for creative work.

  ▶ In your community, there may be a reserve of resources, assets, talents, gifts, and the like that if leveraged as a common fund, could create an interesting, creative, and community-centered pool to sustain and cultivate flourishing for everyone. It may not be a tool library, but that is an idea you and others can riff on in your own neighborhood.

  ▶ Investigating ways that common resource pools can go beyond charitable giving to creatively spur economic opportunity is one of the biggest practical takeaways we can suggest that arise from the spirit of the gleaning laws. How might you creatively leverage a common pool of resources to create genuine opportunity for neighbors to fashion a future for themselves?

- Analyze and eliminate control mechanisms in the resource flow. Gleaning ethics seriously challenge the control exerted by the wealthier members of a community on those on the lower end of the socioeconomic spectrum. In many ways, this is an organizational concern. Churches, nonprofits, and others should audit their practices to find ways in which power and control might be needlessly heavy.

▶ So who are the decision makers for resource sharing? What kinds of policies shape the way resources get shared? Do those policies foster the exchange of resources, or do they restrict resource flow? Do people have a voice in systems that impact them?

▶ Being ruthlessly honest about policies, practices, and postures that reinforce unhealthy power dynamics is a direct implication of the ethical framework gleaning offers us.

SEVEN

SABBATH: AN ECONOMY
OF RESTORATION

In chapter 4, we considered Sabbath ethics as a way of promoting restoration of people, land, and community. This is the essence of the work in the neighborhood today. When we think about how to nurture the ethics of Sabbath, we are looking for ways to prioritize restoration. We want to bring our best thinking to how we might creatively enact restoration through economic practices and projects. That restoration is thoroughgoing; it includes individuals, families, neighborhood blocks, the land itself, and the culture and community fostered in the places we call home together.

Sabbath ethics are also an expansion of the ethics of gleaning. Because Sabbath ethics foster a restorative economy, they will necessarily include those who are on the margins or excluded. In practice, gleaning and Sabbath work together, not as distinct agendas but as a fuller picture of an economic way of life in community that resists the damage done by both exclusion and extraction.

As we explore how we might nurture the economic ethics of Sabbath today, we begin with the story of Philemon, or rather what we understand of the story through Paul's letter to Philemon, regarding his slave Onesimus. As Paul wrote to Philemon and sent Onesimus—who had run away from slavery under Philemon—back to him, the letter underscores Paul's commitment to the ethics of Sabbath and the vision of Jesus's Jubilee. In short, Paul was inviting Philemon not only not to punish Onesimus for running to Paul but to go beyond that and free Onesimus from slavery as an expression of the demands of the gospel and Christian community.

Paul understood that the gospel created a mandate for liberation of Onesimus. The Sabbath demand for restoration over extraction is noteworthy as Paul told Philemon that his days of profiting off the labor of Onesimus were done. Paul said, "In Christ I could be bold and order you to do what you ought to do" (Philemon 8), which we come to understand is related to Philemon setting Onesimus free. Here is the reality that everything is always being set free in Christ in practice. This is not a spiritual abstraction or a future hope alone, but a concrete expression of the good news of Jesus. Paul said that in releasing Onesimus, Philemon can now receive Onesimus into the community as a brother, not as a slave. The liberation of Christ redefines the way relationships work in practice. In Christ, Christians are called to reject the social arrangements of economic extraction and instead restore the harmony of relationship between people, land, and community. Paul finished the letter by telling Philemon that he was "confident of [his] obedience" (v. 21), again highlighting the reality that there was an expectation of conformity to the new reality of Christ's kingdom.

It is also worth noting a few smaller ideas that connect some threads we've established already. First, the reason Paul didn't actually force the liberation of Onesimus is not because it was optional, but because Philemon needed to do the work himself. Authentic restoration of Onesimus and long-term viability of those redefined relations depended on Philemon making this move. Onesimus's freedom depended on Philemon, but as Paul reminded him, Philemon's fidelity to Christ and the demands of the gospel depended on his conformity to the compulsion of liberation. Paul's consistent nod to the fact that he *could* order him do this was an assurance that while active participation on Philemon's part was the surest way to bring about good results, gospel compulsion was not out of the realm of possibility.

Second, Paul offered to pay any cost Philemon incurred in order to assure the liberation of Onesimus, saying, "Charge it to me" (v. 18). At first glance, this runs counter to the notion of restoration—paying off slaveholders to ensure the freedom of those they enslaved. But there may be more to this offer when we consider that Paul was demonstrating a deep solidarity with Onesimus, calling him his "son" (v. 10) who "is my very heart" (v. 12). Paul's willingness to give his own resources to ensure the liberation of the vulnerable Onesimus was an expression of openhandedness and a recognition that there is a concrete financial cost associated with standing alongside the marginalized and advocating for their liberation.

Third, Paul said in closing that he was sure that Philemon

would "do even more than I ask" (v. 21). Here is a nod to abundance and an allusion to the sharing of wealth that comes with debt release of the Sabbath year. The ethics of Sabbath counter a culture of extraction through concrete expressions of abundance as a marker of the restoration of, in this case, Onesimus to the community.

As we consider how we might begin to piece together a framework for embodying Sabbath ethics today in such a way that we nurture a restorative economy, we do well to begin with an image Paul provided in this text when he said, "Welcome [Onesimus] as you would welcome me" (v. 17). Obviously, Onesimus had been gone, so Paul had a concrete "return" in mind, but as we tease out the metaphor of welcome, we might expand the notion to welcoming back those who have been excluded from the community.

Onesimus's slave status left him on the margins because he had become an object of extraction. This, of course, is the natural result of extraction. People and places are used for the extraction of profit until no more profit can be extracted, at which point they are discarded or excluded. This is the ultimate end of all extractive processes, and we see the results of this disregard in people and places too casually cast aside as society exhausts its imagination for how to continue to profit from them.

But Paul countered the notion that Onesimus was a body to extract profit from as he advocated for Onesimus's new identity within the community. He was not a slave; he was a brother. In welcoming Onesimus back, Philemon had an opportunity to embrace the redefinition of social relations and to practice a kind of prophetic inclusion that restores people to authentic membership in the community. Here is evidence that a restorative economy brings the ethics of gleaning and Sabbath together as it responds to the injustices of exclusion and extraction at the same time. This is also Jubilee in action as Onesimus was reclaiming his agency over his very self by being set free from slavery.

Restoration of the harmony of people, land, and community cannot be a spiritual notion only. The same way Paul advocated for the working class's inclusion in the community of God in 1 Corinthians 11 through concrete change in the structures of how the community practiced its life together, here Paul argued that authentic gospel expression demands a redefinition of community that is both relational and structural.

So, in reflection, we might say that a restorative economy

- welcomes the excluded by redefining social relationships and advocating for their inclusion,
- challenges practices of economic extraction by creating new systems for economic participation,
- proclaims a gospel mandate for the wealthy to cooperate with Christ's liberation of the poor through opening their hands in generous abundance, and
- integrates both economic and environmental justice into a vision for the gospel.

Restoring People

In South Bend, Indiana, Jeff Walker is the executive director of Beacon Community Resource Center, a nonprofit that has historically partnered with other organizations attempting to foster some renewed vitality in the city. For the last decade or so, the center functioned as a shared-space model for the west side, which had a relative dearth of safe and accessible space for community gatherings and programming. Over the last few years, Jeff began to observe ways that South Bend could practice a more restorative economy, particularly related to those returning from prison.

Neighbors returning to society after incarceration encounter serious obstacles to flourishing in community. While dealing with the social stigma that comes with a criminal record, returning citizens face significant economic challenges related to securing housing, obtaining/keeping a job and income stream, and finding reliable and affordable transportation. At the same time, they often have to manage a complex and rigidly unforgiving parole system, which can also include significant costs to pay for monitoring systems and the like. In a world that views returning citizens as objects of economic extraction, the fact that private companies profit off the parole system is merely an extension of the private prison industrial complex.

The economic pressures of life after incarceration are one of the primary reasons for recidivism. In short, we do not "welcome back" returning citizens to our communities; instead, we have systems, structures, and social stigmas in place that exclude our neighbors, leaving a vulnerable population of folks to fend for themselves in a society shaped to keep them marginalized while simultaneously building systems to continue to extract profit from their presence in the community.

Jeff, among others, has a different vision for the city. His organization hosts a yearly event focused on raising awareness around the issues of mass incarceration and the plight faced by neighbors returning from time in prison. At this event, stories are told of the incredible work happening in the city among all manner of partners and practitioners, including mass expungement clinics and innovative business models, that attempt to mitigate some of the barriers faced by returning citizens. These events advocate for the community, specifically the Christian community, to reframe the way returning citizens are viewed and treated and highlight ways the systems still exclude and prevent a genuine welcome that can lead to deep restoration. Jeff has a vision for the city that would change the way folks relate to the formerly incarcerated. This vision is rooted in the gospel reality of inherent human dignity and the implications of grace when applied to the systems and structures of the city. The work integrates an application of the gospel, as well as—remembering Philemon—the expectation that the gospel compels the people of God toward a more radical form of redemptive inclusion.

That advocacy extends beyond the public event as Jeff works with local organizers to promote solutions to over-incarceration in the community. Recognizing that finding a job after incarceration is difficult, Jeff is building a network of "second-chance-friendly" employers by giving business owners a vision for a flourishing community that welcomes the formerly incarcerated and challenges them to identify and remove the barriers to employment within their companies. The fruit of that work has been a series of job fairs specifically designed for returning citizens, with employers committed to providing next-chance employment opportunities, including some companies thinking strategically and specifically about the economic inclusion of returning citizens. This is one way the asset rich in the community are practicing a redemptive generosity toward these returning neighbors.

Creating this system for finding work has opened up other opportunities to provide support for returning citizens attempting to navigate the community, but it has also exposed other systems that exclude. Jeff and others are working on, among other things, housing solutions for those who either can't return to their original residence for whatever reason or can't secure the capital needed to find sustainable housing on their own. The work of advocating for fuller inclusion of returning citizens has developed into a keen sense of discernment for ways we continue to, intentionally or not, exclude our neighbors from the harmony of life in community.

Jeff and Beacon are good examples of how the four principles we teased out from the New Testament church can be applied in concrete ways in our communities today. These stories are the fruit of what we might call a growing restorative imagination within the people of God, a key component in our collective capacity to practice Sabbath ethics. A communal imagination for restoration is one marked by an eager and creative curiosity about what our community might look like if it were restored, if it were released from its "bondage to decay" (Rom. 8:21). Discovering and honing a communal vision for those notions can lead to productive conversation around what might be done to participate in creating concrete economic practices of restoration.

Restoring Community

As we have noted, one of the challenges in economically disadvantaged communities is the temptation for outside interests to see the community as having asset-rich potential without concern for the restoration of the community itself. At one level, these outside eyes see what we want everyone to see—the asset potential of particular neighborhoods. However, very often those assets can be extracted and the real value of the asset is not realized by the people in the neighborhood. Local groups can imagine new economic engines that help communities realize the asset potential of their own resources and, in so doing, push back against the forces of extraction that threaten the harmony of the neighborhood ecosystem. Getting clear on the resources and potential assets of your community is a good first step to then start ideating economic tactics to create greater economic health in the neighborhood. But we then need to consider creative economic interventions that resist extraction.

So if we are working on revitalizing homes in a community, can we create projects that simultaneously promote local ownership (Jubilee!) so that the economic fruit of home ownership (money for schools, etc.) is realized in the neighborhood? Can we create strategies for restoring the community that resist gentrification—like serious income limits that help asset-depleted neighbors qualify for homes? Of course, groups all over are experimenting with various models and adapting their work to be more effective. There is much we can gain from folks doing work in their local spaces.

We might also identify ways to make abandoned commercial

spaces available for the community to help launch ideas that create revenue streams for the neighborhood from outside (the original intention of the pie shop). Beyond that, we might consider ways of restoring commercial spaces to support local entrepreneurs as well. This has implications for Jubilee and ownership, but it also creates ways to attract and keep neighbors in the neighborhood.

Retaining talent (resisting talent extraction) in a neighborhood is an important part of nurturing a restorative economy as well. The extractive practices are reinforced by stories that encourage people with talent, education, and relative financial resources to leave for a "better place." This talent drain leaves neighborhood ecosystems vulnerable to the impacts of poverty. In her book *Reclaiming Your Community*, Majora Carter describes how there is a narrative gap that happens early with young people that reinforces talent drain in our neighborhoods. Talent drain is when people move out of communities and take their social, economic, and intellectual capital elsewhere because they have the capacity to do so. Carter's company was able to perform its own assessment in the South Bronx, the poorest urban congressional district. The results indicated that people didn't necessarily leave because of high crime rates but because of a vision that lacked diversity and dimension for its residents across the class spectrum. She asks, "What if we designed . . . communities to encourage the talent born and raised there to remain, similar to the way companies try to retain their talent?"[1] Majora sees the South Bronx as a "gleaning field" with hidden assets in people. Finding ways to retain the middle class is key; those with means are important for the economic diversity of the ecosystem. And it is one of the ways to cultivate talents to combat the narrative of extraction. Majora further writes, "You need more economic diversity, not less of it, to reverse the cycle that maintains high poverty levels. . . . Everything we know about diversity applies to the economic ecosystem that governs the built environment of [disinherited] communities."[2]

Restoring Land

Admittedly, much of this book has been written with urban, or urbanizing, spaces in mind. Given the context of the majority of our work, our natural inclination is to narrate this vision for Jubilee economics with city life in mind. And there is a disconnect at times between those advocating for justice in urban spaces and those advocating for environmental justice issues. We've tried throughout this project to draw our attention to the inherent interconnectivity between people, the land, and flourishing communities because it can be easy to overlook the need for land restoration, or at least to see restoring the land as a separate issue from urban economic justice.

However, Sabbath ethics give us a clear way to reintegrate a vision for economic justice—in cities and elsewhere—with a vision for stewarding the land on which we give shape to more flourishing communities. Through the lens of Sabbath, we come to see the land as an actor in the story of God's shalom and, as we have noted, a victim of the same kind of economic extraction experienced by people on the economic margins—extending from ancient Israel until today. English farmer James Rebanks writes that "the whole history of farming was really the story of people trying and often failing to overcome natural constraints on production. . . . Farmers learned the hard way through endless experimentation, trial and error, discovering that if we overexploited our soil, ecosystems would collapse, and our ability to live and prosper with it."[3] Unrestrained extraction from the land, in pursuit of overcoming the natural limits of production, nurtures unhealthy ecosystems and destroys harmony between people, land, and the community being created between the two.

We argue this is particularly true in cities, despite the fact that land is often disconnected from the discussion of economic justice in urban spaces. For example, low-income communities are often full of degraded buildings—abandoned homes, vacant lots, and boarded-up storefronts—evidence of both economic calamity and the effects of economic extraction. These so-called eyesores are the fruit of suburbanization and the economic consequences of extractive business practices over the last few generations. They are in neighborhoods that have been excluded from the larger economic life, and so the people who remain live under a kind of double threat of economic vulnerability. Often they are trapped in depreciating assets without means to improve conditions and, as we mentioned earlier, can be seen as a potential economic opportunity for gentrification. The restoration and reinvigoration of those physical spaces, designed for the benefit of the folks who live in the community, help to bring economic stability to a community but also offer a prophetic word of challenge that no place should exist outside the harmony of community. Collaboration with others toward these ends is a straightforward way of fostering a more restorative economy.

Additionally, these neighborhoods often deal with serious environmental hazards that stem from that same economic neglect. They are more likely to deal with issues like lead in their homes and ground that contaminates living space, food, and water, leaving young children to suffer the majority of the consequences. Oftentimes, these communities also deal with larger environmental hazard conditions—in some cases because of the neglect of companies long gone from the community. These environmental hazards only magnify issues like racialized health disparities and further economic challenges as people's homes are now—sometimes literally—radioactive and there is no means of selling/relocating to healthier environments. Environmental restoration takes Sabbath ethics seriously by seeking to restore the land itself, but when that work is coupled with restoration of economically vulnerable communities, the impact is magnified as it helps reintegrate the neighborhood into the larger economic ecosystem.

The environmental threats faced by people and places in our communities are not only dormant or the result of historical neglect. Low-income neighborhoods are often under siege by industries that degrade the environment and create health risks to community residents. Because of the cheap land available adjacent to low-income communities, industrial zones often pop up and pollute critical systems necessary for healthy living. Air quality concerns, contaminated water, and unjust disparities related to diseases like cancer are a real concern in the communities we are writing about. In this case, it is not just a matter of cleaning up and restoring the damage done. Sabbath ethics invite us to see that our work includes advocating for the land and the people who live on it, and to resist the extractive forces of environmentally dangerous industry—in its own right, but particularly when in proximity to the poor and vulnerable. For example, St. James Parish, just outside New Orleans, is in a region colloquially, and tragically, referred to as "cancer alley." This is due to the massive environmental degradation largely caused by petro-chemical companies that dot the landscape. Prolonged exposure to emissions and environmental contamination has caused health issues in the region to skyrocket. An organization called Rise St. James is advocating for environmental justice on behalf of the people of the community.[4] Their work helps mobilize citizens and aims to organize against the proliferation of industries that poison the ground and exact a huge health toll on the most vulnerable. They see their work as an expression of faith. We see their work as an expression of Sabbath ethics in action.

Reintegrating the land into our vision for what it means to practice economic justice in our neighborhoods is essential work. We can practice Sabbath ethics in ways big and small. We can, as the prophet Jeremiah called Israel to do in Babylon, plant our own gardens and eat what they produce. We can resist large-scale, environmentally unconcerned agriculture and buy our produce from local farmers who practice restorative agriculture. We can collaborate with friends and neighbors to develop community gardens in unused spaces— perhaps vacant lots can become guerrilla gardens and spaces for community connection. We can organize neighborhood cleanups. We can form groups to do low-level lead remediation for families dealing with unsafe conditions in their homes. We can reimagine uses for abandoned commercial spaces and spark economic revitalization that keeps the neighborhood in mind. All these examples are happening in my (Adam's) city. In nearly every case, these movements began by ordinary people taking seriously their role as neighbors, and—whether they knew it or not—they enacted the ethics of Sabbath by seeking the harmony of the people, the land, and the community.

Getting Started with Sabbath

Gleaning practices focus on the asset holders loosening their grip, and the discernment work is focused on opportunities for the rich to repent of being tightfisted. Sabbath, on the other hand, focuses our discernment and work in a different direction. Here are a few ways to start working out the ethics of Sabbath:

- Identify and name both the exclusions and the extractions. Who, in particular, is being excluded from participation and why? Your neighborhood may not have a large population of returning citizens, but surely there are some within the community who are not just being overlooked but are actively and systemically being excluded from participation. Understanding the particular nature of that exclusion is essential work if we want to nurture an economic life that restores folks to full inclusion. Similarly, get specific about what resources are being extracted and how the resource and asset potential of your neighborhood is being extracted from individuals and the community at large. How are the poor and vulnerable being victimized for profit? Is it predatory lending? Vacant and dishonest landlords? Low-wage and demeaning work? Similarly, are outside agents tapping into the potential of your neighborhood flourishing and realizing the profits elsewhere? Are there resource flows leading out of the neighborhood rather than into your neighborhood?

- That work can lead to spaces for moral leadership and advocacy for those on the margins. Very likely that leadership is in place and advocacy is happening in at least small ways already. Find the folks doing the work and support and collaborate with them. Bring a faith-filled perspective if it is not there already.

- Find and join collective efforts to protect the ecological health of your community. Doubtless there are ways in which ecological harm is creating hazards for your neighborhood (lead poisoning is a good example and is common in many communities). Restoring ecological health as neighbors—particularly in ways that protect the most vulnerable in the community—is a great way to practice inclusion and restoration at the same time.

- Practice Sabbath rhythms in secular spaces. Sabbath in the Old Testament was not just about spiritual renewal but about social renewal that included protections for economically vulnerable folks; thus, modern-day Sabbath practices must necessarily extend into the broader public sphere. Are there ways to gather as a community for restoration that protects the need for the poor to be restored and to re-create as much as the rich?

EIGHT

JUBILEE: AN ECONOMY OF OWNERSHIP AND CELEBRATION

Nearing the close of the Civil War, General William Tecumseh Sherman issued a directive, Special Field Order 15 (SFO 15) that famously made "40 acres and a mule" available to newly freed slaves. As a straightforward expression of reparations for slavery, this was, at face value, a revolutionary response coming from the Emancipation Proclamation of 1863. Some four hundred thousand acres of land were parceled out to newly freed people, mostly on the coast and outlying areas of the Carolinas. Notably, these were lands historically owned by some of the "wealthiest segments of the planter class."[1] Having considered all we have thus far, it's not too difficult to read the ethics of Jubilee into the particulars of Sherman's directive.

However, SFO 15 was not as magnanimous—nor aimed at justice—as one may imagine. Sherman did not intend the land grant to be permanent; instead, it was aimed at "relieving the immediate pressure caused by the large number of impoverished blacks following his army."[2] That the land was wrested from the possession of Southern elites undoubtedly proved to be one of the many ways Sherman sought to exact retribution on the Confederacy, and that it allowed free Blacks "land, upon which they might locate their families and work out for themselves a living and respectability,"[3] seemed to be more a matter of crisis management than an enactment of justice.

Still, the move was significant, if only for the fact that it was precipitated by Sherman gathering Black community leaders, mostly ministers, in Savannah to ask their thoughts on the situation. Eric Foner tells the story of that gathering in his book *Reconstruction: America's Unfinished Revolution 1863–1877*:

> The conversation revealed that these black leaders possessed a clear conception of the meaning of freedom. Asked what he understood by slavery, Garrison Frazer, a Baptist minister who had known bondage for 60 years before purchasing his freedom in 1857, responded that it meant "receiving . . . the work of another man, and not by his consent." Freedom he defined as "placing us where we could reap the fruit of our own labor"; the best way to accomplish this was "to have land, and turn it and till it by our own labor.[4]

It is interesting to note that the basic framework of SFO 15 was conceived by Black ministers. It suggests that something in the theological imagination of historically oppressed peoples—so often shaped by Israel's own story of liberation from Egypt and deliverance to a promised land—intuits that liberation and land are inextricably tied together. The end of war and violence, coupled with the liberation of people, naturally creates the need for the oppressed to come into possession of their own land. Ownership, as Minister Frazier noted, was essential to the flourishing of newly liberated peoples. Remembering the discussion on Sabbath, simply releasing the debt of slavery does not ensure flourishing; instead, liberation should be accompanied by asset ownership to avoid creating a continuing state of unnecessary economic vulnerability.

Unfortunately, SFO 15 did not turn out to be the liberation these ministers had hoped for. Aside from Sherman's utilitarian approach, the livestock provided to families on these plots of ground were loans rather than given assets and, in a particularly cruel expression of how economic forces and white supremacy go hand in hand, the provisions of SFO 15 were undone by Andrew Johnson a few years later, and the land was returned to the planter classes that had extracted so much profit off the backs of these Black women, men, and their ancestors over generations. Instead of an economic reset that prioritized the long-term well-being of the historically oppressed, "40 acres and a mule" proved little more than a stopgap in the continual onslaught of racialized economic exploitation.

The legacy of Special Field Order 15 was a far cry from the vision shared in that meeting with Black pastors. These ministers from Savannah had proposed a solution in the spirit of the prophets. These ministers echoed the vision of Isaiah, who declared God's promise of renewal and justice, saying,

> See, I will create
> new heavens and a new earth.

The former things will not be remembered,
 nor will they come to mind.
But be glad and rejoice forever
 in what I will create,
for I will create Jerusalem to be a delight
 and its people a joy.
I will rejoice over Jerusalem
 and take delight in my people;
the sound of weeping and of crying
 will be heard in it no more.

Never again will there be in it
 an infant who lives but a few days,
 or an old man who does not live out his years;
the one who dies at a hundred
 will be thought a mere child;
the one who fails to reach a hundred
 will be considered accursed.
They will build houses and dwell in them;
 they will plant vineyards and eat their fruit.
No longer will they build houses and others live
  in them,
 or plant and others eat.
For as the days of a tree,
 so will be the days of my people;
my chosen ones will long enjoy
 the work of their hands. (Isa. 65:17–22)

Isaiah's words highlight a new day—a day when all will be made right, including the reality that the people will not be exploited for their labor; they will not produce the fruit of someone else's vine. This is similar to a text we considered earlier, where we read about Micah's prophetic proclamation of a world set to rights by the Messiah:

> Come, let us go up to the mountain of the LORD,
>> to the temple of the God of Jacob. . . .
> He will judge between many peoples
>> and will settle disputes for strong nations far
>> and wide.
> They will beat their swords into plowshares
>> and their spears into pruning hooks.
> Nation will not take up sword against nation,
>> nor will they train for war anymore.
> Everyone will sit under their own vine
>> and under their own fig tree,
> and no one will make them afraid,
>> for the LORD Almighty has spoken. (4:2–4)

In this text, we see similar elements to Reconstruction and the goals of Black leaders in Savannah. Micah speaks of a messianic liberation marked by the end of violence and war and the striking line "Everyone will sit under their own vine and under their own fig tree, and no one will make them afraid." Micah's messianic vision makes the same claim as the ministers in 1863. Everyone will have their own land on which to till and toil, making something of it for themselves. They will not live in fear, for there will be no threats to their well-being. In the messianic vision of the prophets, everyone is free to flourish because liberation and land are tied together.

Jubilee Today

How do we practice Jubilee in the neighborhood? In Scripture, the release of slaves, debt forgiveness, and return of land are intertwined to help us see the interrelatedness of people, land, and a thriving community as essential to the harmony of all. But that's not nearly as easy to envision today, either in our modern society or at the local level. As we've already seen, the Year of Jubilee had two fundamental elements. Jubilee dealt with the question of ownership and saw equitable ownership distribution as a check on exploitation and injustice. Jubilee was also a celebration, a joyous festival-like declaration of God's goodness and provision. As we seek to give expression to Jubilee in the neighborhood, we want to keep those two ideas in view.

So, to start, the practice of Jubilee helps reframe our perspective on ownership. God frames the land as God's own possession, given as a gift to steward, which invites owners to see the land (and all their assets) in a new light. In other words, *because it is God's, it is not mine.* At the same time, Jubilee called for the land to be returned to the original tribe, a group of people that owned the land as more of a collective trust. This adds further texture to the way owners see their land: *because it is ours, it is not mine.* At no point is the land free to be seen as the private, sole, and permanent possession of an individual or family. The health of the ecosystem depends on individual "owners" seeing their task as one of stewardship among the community of God.

At the same time, Jubilee is also a celebration. The Year of Jubilee was intended to be a celebration woven into the fabric of the people's calendar of feasts and festivals that marked God's faithfulness by reminding and rehearsing the historic action of God all the while fostering an expectant hope in the future justice of God. That particular actions of economic liberation (slaves, debt, land) were prescribed for the people on the basis of such a celebration is instructive. Celebration carries with it an expectation of a way of life that gives tangible expression to that which is being celebrated. In that regard, we think that Jubilee as a celebration of liberation is a helpful way of framing the work of practicing Jubilee.

It may seem strange to consider the practice of Jubilee the work of developing an economy of celebration, so we want to add one additional layer to the way we understand celebration. There is a sense in which, theologically speaking, celebration, like Jubilee, is eschatological. As we mentioned, the celebrations of God's people in the Old Testament were opportunities to proclaim God's faithfulness in the past and look forward expectantly to God's faithfulness in the future. There is an eschatological texture to the intersection of remembrance and expectation. As that intersection creates a particular pattern of life that manifests in celebration and concrete action on behalf of the poor, dispossessed, and defortuned, we find ourselves in the imaginative space of Jubilee.

Practicing Jubilee today means finding ways to foster a community of eschatological celebration in the neighborhood and make direct connections between liberation of the oppressed and their participation and agency in the neighborhood. We are invited to "reach back" and honor the ethics and aspirations of the Old Testament people of God who looked toward a day when God would make everything right.

Practicing Jubilee involves honoring those hopes of Israel, who envisioned a society where everyone (even the poor) would own and cultivate land without fear. The fruition of that vision is evidence of God's economy at work, evidence of the rich having opened their hands, and evidence of the work of God, who topples empires in favor of the lowly. This calls for celebration because—as we've already seen—it is evidence of how everything is always being set free.

We are likewise invited to take Jesus seriously when he proclaimed a new era of Jubilee. Declaring the year of the Lord's favor in Luke 4 was like a trumpet blast that Israel's aspirations had come to fruition in him. The status quo of society was being interrupted by the inbreaking of that eschatological reality. We are invited to give practical expression to that reality as a proclamation that the intentions of God have been established once and for all in Christ. In the same way the eschatological vision of the prophets called the people toward justice then, the proclamation of Jesus and the vision of a renewed creation invite us into a particular way of life now.

Extending Ownership and Practicing Celebration

If liberation and land are tied together, we foster Jubilee in the neighborhood by recognizing the essential connection between asset ownership and individual and community flourishing. This may seem to clash with our earlier argument for the need to reenvision privatized ownership, but they are, as we see it, necessary points of tension. Ownership in the scriptural tradition had a character of stewardship to it, a caretaking texture that recognized God's ultimate sovereignty over the land. That is not exactly how we think of ownership today, and reclaiming that perspective helps us navigate that tension. So the wealthy need to reimagine their view of ownership, and asset accumulation, if they want to meaningfully contribute to the health of their community ecosystems. That reimagining should be aimed at creatively conceiving ways to expand *access* to ownership among those who are particularly vulnerable economically. This is the Jubilee reset.[5] When we said, in chapter 1, that Jubilee is freedom for the rich and poor alike, we have this notion in view. Theologically speaking, equitable asset ownership, and the work of collaborating to creatively cultivate those assets among the economically vulnerable, is Jubilee in action.

This is just another way all three economic ethics find a singular expression. Equitable asset ownership enacts the spirit of gleaning, as it involves the rich opening their hands and freeing the edges of their fields for the poor to make use of. It creates a community ethos where, because ownership is increasingly distributed across the rich-poor divide, everyone is welcome and everyone has access to the economic life of the community. The ethics of Sabbath are expressed in the refusal to view land or assets as opportunities for economic extraction. Ownership enacts the Jubilee vision of a community where people are set free from indebtedness to the wealthy and instead contribute not only toward their own well-being but also to the well-being of the entire community. Gleaning and Sabbath draw us naturally into the practice of Jubilee. Jubilee completes the triad of economic ethics and gives us the fullest picture of God's intent for the ecosystems of human community.

A Jubilee Ecosystem in Brightmoor

The Brightmoor neighborhood in Detroit is full of examples of things people might point out to reinforce generations-old stereotypes about the city. Many parts of Detroit are prime examples of the toll that economic exclusion, extraction, and overt injustice can take on once-thriving communities, and there are significant challenges to reinvigorate the neighborhood ecosystems of the city.

Yet, amid the challenge, there are stories of the kingdom of God, or the Great Economy, in action. Pastor Semmeal and City Covenant Church have been faithfully caring for their community for many years, engaging in good, traditional forms of ministry and an ongoing and faithful demonstration of love and concern for folks on the margins. Their community meals—served daily!—pack out the church fellowship hall and, over time, City Covenant has become a hub—not just for economic hospice care but for creative and transformative engagement in their neighborhood. Pastor Semmeal had a vision for the purchase and renovation of blighted homes in the neighborhood; with a small starter grant from some collaborators, the church purchased homes and renovated them to provide affordable housing for their neighbors. A home-by-home approach began to bear fruit as folks in the community found some residential stability, and the model was sustained as each house was sold to folks in the neighborhood.

This is a wonderful example of the connection between assets and liberation to be sure, but what makes Pastor Semmeal's work stand out is the way in which he envisioned the larger ecosystem at work. Instead of thinking about this project as merely housing, Semmeal saw it as an opportunity to jump-start the natural talents and experiences of folks in his church and neighborhood who had, for whatever reason, found themselves unemployed or underemployed. Local tradespeople were hired for specific jobs. Folks with experience as contractors received help to restart their businesses to manage the projects. New businesses—like security companies—owned by people in the community sprung up to support the work. Building on that, the church collaborated with other congregations to create a common fund (gleaning!) out of which they could make microloans and provide business coaching to start-up businesses all over the neighborhood. A relatively small amount of money has helped launch over twenty new businesses in the span of just a few years. City Covenant is not an asset-rich congregation. Pastor Semmeal says, "We are a poor church . . . but it's about relationships, partnerships, and collaborations." Whether your church, organization, or community group has resources or not, there is a role you can play in this work.

What started as a vision for affordable housing alone became something much more. The resources injected into housing work helped to generate new work around the community; it is a real example of the "underground" in action and of the ways flourishing can be shared among many. Pastor Semmeal is helping the ecosystem of Brightmoor by creating a business ecosystem that continually expands its impact in the community.

Transform Capital—A Communal Celebration of Ownership

In North Chicago, an economically vulnerable community surrounded by Fortune 500 company headquarters and suburbs of incredible wealth, many families struggle to gain a foothold in homeownership. The community has experienced much of the economic injustice we've explored throughout this book: disinvestment, exclusion, and a long history of discrimination and economic crisis. The community is majority Black and brown, further distinguishing it from the wealthy communities around it, many of whom live in substandard housing. Yet North Chicago is a community rich in resources and assets and in many ways is representative of the communities we've had in mind as we've written this book.

Transform Capital is a nonprofit lending initiative led by faith-filled folks from communities surrounding the North Chicago area. Recognizing the gifts present in the community, and the patterns of continued injustice in much of what passes as charitable giving and inner-city investment, the leaders of Transform Capital have envisioned an alternative system of exchange that prioritizes ownership in North Chicago.

Transform Capital (they call themselves the TC community) notes that their vision is "investment in human flourishing," which "makes no cents."[6] The deliberate play on words indicates their strategy of investment in people, in which profit potential is not an opportunity to build wealth for the wealthy but a means of nurturing the further vitality of the community itself. Their model depends on recycled capital, as their home loan program has created a self-sustaining current of resources that are channeled to new homeowners in North Chicago. Low interest rates and forgivable down payment programs further enable long-excluded families to participate in an economic system that can create generational wealth, which also nurtures a more thriving local ecosystem in North Chicago.

What's more, the TC community sees itself as just that—a

community. The work of creating local homeowners is also repairing the breach of harmony between people in a new community. To paraphrase Dietrich Bonhoeffer, the TC community is a space where homeownership is setting people free to be in relationship with others in new ways. Remembering Sabbath, the TC community is redefining social relationships by creating systems of inclusion. In the TC community, it is easy to see why homeownership is, in the spirit of Jubilee, a cause for celebration. The TC community evidences the link we read about in the Old Testament that land (ownership) and liberation are bound together. And because Jubilee is a celebration, the TC community celebrates the many people who become part of the work; it is a space where the gifts, talents, and personhood of a person are a cause for celebration.

Freeing the Land for the People

Coté Soerens is a Latina businesswoman, community organizer, and coplanter of the South Park Neighborhood Church. For years, she and her husband, Tim, have worked with the neighborhood to see its economy flourish. South Park is a neighborhood that has suffered the impact of historic redlining and racialized zoning, with nearly one third of the neighborhood living below the poverty line.

For Coté, part of seeking the shalom of South Park has been working to keep neighborhood property in the hands of South Park residents. These efforts included cofounding Cultivate South Park, an organization dedicated to asset community development. Cultivate South Park recognizes shared ownership of the neighborhood as a more just way to flourishing. Meanwhile, preventing prospectors who don't have the community's interests at heart remains the challenge of neighborhood development. Through years of negotiating, fundraising, and planning, Cultivate South Park was able to acquire thirty-two thousand square feet in the downtown area of South Park in partnership with the Cultural Space Agency.

Coté said, "The purchase of this property is a jubilee moment for South Park and a sign of hope for Seattle. It shows what's possible when residents organize to reclaim their communities and co-create a more equitable place with hope and care for everyone in the barrio."[7] What makes this acquisition distinct is the actions taken to give the community actual ownership stake in the property. To fulfill this, they created The Barrio Trust, an agency that will ensure that the neighbors in the community can be investors in the property as well.

Currently on the property is historic South Park Hall, which has been put to immediate use since the land purchase. South Park Hall hosts community events and provides affordable space to the neighborhood for special occasions. Also on the property is the South Park Idea Lab, a coworking space, and a few locally owned businesses, including Resistencia Coffee, a coffee shop founded by Coté and Tim. *Resistancia* means resistance, and in true Jubilee fashion, they are blessing the South Park community by providing pathways to local ownership of the neighborhood.

Getting Started with Jubilee

What's stopping us from fostering an imagination like Pastor Semmeal's in our neighborhoods? Or gathering resource-rich folks with a heart to practice economic justice to imagine

195

interventions like the Transform Capital Community? Or organizing friends and neighbors for a movement animated by the spirit of Jubilee like Cultivate South Park and Resistencia?

Admittedly, the ethical invitations of gleaning and Sabbath are easier to step into than Jubilee. Because the framework we are building takes on the complexity of asset ownership with Jubilee, the examples we shared are not things we can just start up on a typical Monday morning. These are examples born out of years of experience fostering the ethical imagination of the gleaning-Sabbath-Jubilee triad and by building significant collaborative relationships through a long-term commitment to place and people. In that sense, the only way to "get to" Jubilee is to take gleaning and Sabbath seriously right now, from now on. At the same time, economic justice—seen through the Jubilee lens—is truly a work of all the people, not just those reading this book and hoping for some good ideas. So we want to suggest a few ways to start thinking about Jubilee, and acting Jubilee-like, as a long-term pathway to enacting Jubilee.

- Expand our appreciation and participation in feasts and festivals. If you've lived in a city for any length of time, you know that ethnic and neighborhood festivals are highlights of the summer. Engaging with these festivals and creatively curating new opportunities to celebrate with neighbors in ways that highlight the inherent gifts (assets) of the people is the kind of disciplined approach to neighboring that can widen our imagination for ways we might celebrate the connection between people, land, and community.
- Become better storytellers. Jubilee was enacted with a

trumpet blast, a proclamation, and celebration of a new day. Storytelling—in various mediums—is a powerful way to proclaim ways Jubilee is expressed. Finding ways, as neighbors, to tell the stories of the good fruit born from these economic ethics (perhaps as part of regular celebrations and festivals) creates an expectation for more (the aim of all eschatological proclamations) of the same.

- Celebrate asset ownership. House blessings, ribbon cuttings for local businesses, and other formal ceremonies give us space to consider ways we might celebrate with our neighbors the increased distribution of asset ownership in the community. If the prophet Micah thought it was good news that everyone would one day have their own vine and fig tree, we should celebrate the little moments when that reality comes to fruition.

- Consider small experiments that catalyze asset development and opportunity. Similar to the collaboration that Pastor Semmeal had with other local churches, could a small group pool resources to be made available for neighbors with a business plan and a dream?

- Begin to plan, collaborate, and dream. Pastor Semmeal said it best when he noted that the incredible work happening through his community is because of relationships, partnerships, and collaboration. The projects described in this chapter take time, due diligence, and resources. They don't just fall into our laps. Begin talking and dreaming with friends and neighbors about the possibilities that arise when we allow Jubilee to grip our imagination for *what might be* in our neighborhood. You never know what might come up.

BEYOND THE
TWO AMERICAS

Time and again we have turned our attention to the posture, perspective, and personal approach of the wealthy to wealth. And we have noted that in some sense, realizing God's fullest intentions in the neighborhood depend on the participation and cooperation of citizens of the first America. While we both maintain a healthy degree of skepticism about the extent to which justice can be realized when it depends on those who have much to have less, the way of life God instituted for his people seems in fact to make such demands. Rather than throwing up our hands to concede, we must make this discussion of the economic demands placed on the rich an essential part of any vision or strategy for engagement still to come. In other words, it will be very challenging to nurture an ecosystem of Jubilee unless the resource-rich folks take seriously the demands placed on them.

The Prophetic Practice of *Enough*

If there is an economic demand placed on the wealthy by the ethics of gleaning, Sabbath, and Jubilee, it surely comes down to the prophetic practice of *enough* in an all-consuming culture of scarcity and consumption. For example, when the wealthy practice *enough* in strategic ways, they can simultaneously create channels of opportunity for the economically vulnerable to fashion a future for themselves—the intended result of the practice of gleaning. It is worth reminding ourselves that when the wealthy practice gleaning, they are not merely participating in a system of charity. Gleaning is a matter of faithfulness to God rather than an option on the menu of our philanthropy. The same is true for how the practice of *enough* fires our imaginations for ways we might enact the values of Sabbath and Jubilee as well. This is an incredible opportunity to participate in the social and economic reset envisioned by Scripture. That God designed the economic faithfulness of the wealthy to favor the economic fortunes of the poor is something to marvel at—and serves to reinforce the notion of God's preferential option for the poor as discussed in chapter 1.

Admittedly, establishing this mindset can be difficult. Our scarcity culture—breeding scarcity mindsets in each of us—trains us to be afraid of not having enough. We are conditioned to believe that economic calamity lies in wait around each corner, and that the only sane response to that threat is to hoard and hide for oneself and one's own. As we considered in chapter 3, this leads us to close our fists—literally and metaphorically—to the poor, inhibiting our capacity for faithfulness to God and blocking the channel of economic opportunity for the poor. So we must be rigorously committed to discerning the extent to which our fists are closed. When we take an inventory of our economic practices (spending, budgeting, saving, investing, and so on), what conclusions can we draw about our relative open- or closefistedness? Norman Wirzba notes, "If we want to be a Sabbath [and we could add gleaning and Jubilee] people . . . we can start with a fundamental and very practical question: how do we spend our money, and what do our spending patterns say about our trust in God and care for each other?"[1] An audit of our personal finances will reveal more than we'd probably like to know about our posture toward the resources in our hands and whether we faithfully practice God's enough.

Instead of hoarding and hiding, practicing God's *enough* loosens the grip we maintain on "our" margin, setting us free from our bondage to fear and avarice, and gives us the chance to be creative in setting that margin free for the poor to use. This is how we become coparticipants in the cosmic celebration of God's abundance. Seeing our "last-fruits" as the raw material of God's liberative work in the world is an exciting prospect. Learning to let go *expectantly* heightens our anticipation of how these resources might create the opportunity for the flourishing of others. Stewarding resources well to increase the pool available for this kind of work only furthers our own experience of life in a flourishing ecosystem. This allows us to take seriously our capacity to mirror the way environmental ecosystems draw upon the resources of their members as a means of producing ecological harmony and flourishing. It also makes us more aware of the resources others steward that might not show up on a balance sheet. Recognizing the diversity of resources in the hands of each player in God's economy allows us to see better and celebrate the dignity and potential of each of our neighbors—an essential posture of mutuality in community. We stand to gain much if we embrace the prophetic practice of *enough* in a world enslaved to scarcity.

Of course, as we have seen, the fear of scarcity leads to a culture that has a seemingly insatiable appetite for more. Society never pushes back from the table; instead, it believes that a flourishing life and community will be found by spreading the disease of limitless consumption. In her book *Radical Sufficiency*, ethicist Christine Firer Hinze observes that "consumerist culture locks people into the work-spend cycle by imbuing its participants with a chronic sense of scarcity. . . . US-style consumerism perpetrates harms that affect poor and economically vulnerable disproportionately. . . . The consumerist way of life helps sustain and exacerbate economic inequalities."[2] Our consumption drives injustice. Until we learn to say *enough*, those who live at the social margins will always live under economic threat. If we embrace a radical commitment to the value of sufficiency, what we have called enough, we will be "more able to limit acquisitive or consumerist excess when justice or love—for self, family, near and far neighbors, or the earth—requires it."[3]

The question of course is, Are we willing to do it? Are we willing to commit ourselves to this way of being in the world when it comes down to the inevitable tensions we will face when considering how we make use of the resources in our bank accounts and the assets in our possession? Perhaps the greatest word of challenge we can bring, even to ourselves, is to suggest that we cannot contribute to ecosystems of Jubilee in our neighborhoods if we are unwilling to include our personal wealth in the equation. Participation in the work of local, grassroots economic justice will cost us something, according to the logic of the economics of scarcity. It will challenge our deep-seated capitalist notions and cause us to run headlong into conflict with the status quo of the world—a prospect that seems less radical than it will when we find ourselves in tense moments of disagreement with those (perhaps close to us) who simply do not see the value or logic in these actions. It will also challenge any innate desires we may have to be seen as models of generosity and charity, for we will be reminded that our actions are a response to the demands of God on our economic life, and that any social impact that may result is due to the genius inherent in God's intentions for an economic system— and the invitation to participate in that system is an expression of God's grace because that is how we experience real liberation ourselves. In the end, ecosystems of Jubilee depend on the practice of *enough*.

Solidarity Invites Us into the *In-Between*

Throughout this book, we have regularly referred to the relationship between things to describe the precise point of focus for the work of nurturing economic justice. Indeed, the type and quality of the relationships between things is where the health of the local ecosystem will rise and fall. We've pointed to the ideal relationship between people, land, and community as something marked by harmony. We've noted breakdowns in the relationships between people—rich and poor, Black and white, immigrant and citizen—as evidence of the destruction of that harmony. Achieving justice requires that we come to grips with and tend to the in-betweens in our communities. This is Martin Luther King Jr.'s single garment of destiny idea. King called us to see the in-betweens as a fundamental truth. He said, "For some strange reason, I can never be what I ought to be until you are what you ought to be. You can never be what you ought to be until I am what I ought to be. This is the interrelated structure of reality."[4]

Our basic hypothesis is that if two Americas exist, and everything in society has an interrelated structure, then it stands to reason that *between* the two Americas is where the real work of fostering economic justice takes place. Indeed, there is real need to appreciate the way our economic activity is "always embedded in and answerable to cooperative and reciprocal relationships and communities."[5] We must deal with the breakdown in the harmony between the two Americas. Our work is to understand why things are broken and creatively envision ways of restoring the health of the ecosystem. Then, instead of the in-between being characterized by exclusion, extraction, and exploitation, the in-between evidences flourishing in communities increasing in participation, mutuality, and resilience.

We believe that the applied ethics of gleaning, Sabbath, and Jubilee give us an imaginative framework from which to carve out a new approach to local economic life. A healthy neighborhood ecosystem is fostered through people committed to cultivating an economy of sharing, opportunity, restoration, ownership, and celebration. Taken together, we gain vision for what Rebecca Todd Peters calls a "solidarity economy," a "way for first-world Christians to define their obligation to the distant other, to their global neighbor whom they do not know but to whom they are connected through the interdependence of God's created order."[6] A solidarity economy has far-reaching implications. Even though Peters is writing about a global vision for economic solidarity, the implications for our questions are clear. Instead of "first world Christians," we can substitute "citizens of the first America," and note that solidarity helps the wealthy to see both their obligation and connectedness to those on the margins.

Solidarity affirms the idea that "each person is unique in worth and dignity, but no one is on their own. In economic thinking and activity, one's holistic, relational identity as neighbor, friend, family member, colleague, and citizen comes into play."[7] Practicing gleaning, Sabbath, and Jubilee as an interconnected set is a way of enacting economic solidarity.

Solidarity is also tricky. "Undertaking solidarity in the concrete is difficult, messy, and at times scary work."[8] It requires the creation of new relational space. In one way of thinking, solidarity exists only because injustice exists. As Firer Hinze argues, "Solidarity entails a more critical . . . relationship to the status quo."[9] In a perfect world, we would live in community without the need to puzzle out what it means to live in solidarity with one another. That means that we come to the possibility of solidarity from different places. Citizens of the first America occupy a much different social location than do citizens of the second America. For us to practice meaningful solidarity with one another, first America folks will need to engage in serious divestment from the systems and structures that benefit them over others. Second America folks, on the other hand, are not asked to divest. They need the opportunity for greater flourishing. When the downward mobility of first America interacts with increasing economic flourishing of second America, it can create a new possibility for relationships of solidarity. We are free to participate in community life in a manner distinct from the status quo of society. We are free to imagine new possibilities for our neighbors and our neighborhoods. Jubilee is indeed freedom for rich and poor alike, and this is the liberation we all need.

Economic solidarity is, in the end, the mode of being for those committed to fostering a healthy economic ecosystem in their communities. Solidarity as a way of life positions us to embrace, even celebrate, the interconnectedness of our economic life in community. Solidarity pulls even our very persons into the in-between, inviting us out of insular patterns and into new spaces where we can, together, celebrate the reality that everything is always being set free in Christ. God's intentions are meant to be tasted even now, in the most concrete ways, and when we do experience it, we know we are experiencing the fruit of Jesus's life and work, which forever situates our lives in the year of the Lord's favor.

NOTES

Introduction

1. Christopher Wright argues that Jubilee "was an attempt to impede, and indeed periodically reverse, the relentless economic forces that lead to a downward spiral of debt, poverty, dispossession and bondage." Christopher Wright, *An Eye for an Eye* (Downers Grove, IL: InterVarsity Press, 1984), 130, in Lowell Noble, *From Oppression to Jubilee Justice* (Jackson, MS: Urban Verses, 2007), 87.

2. I told parts of this story in my first book, *Becoming a Just Church: Cultivating Communities of God's Shalom* (Downers Grove, IL: InterVarsity, 2019), 77–78, 152–53.

3. Martin Luther King Jr., "The Other America," in *All Labor Has Dignity*, ed. Michael K. Honey (Boston: Beacon, 1986), 156. King gave this speech more than once. The direct quotation here is from his speech in New York City in March 1968.

4. King, "The Other America," 156–57.

5. Iris Marion Young, *Responsibility for Justice* (Oxford: Oxford University Press, 2011). This book is a wonderful collection of essays in which she develops an extensive line of thought in this regard. To that end, I've attempted to frame her overall argument here in my own words while doing justice to the nuance she is presenting.

6. Young, *Responsibility for Justice*, 95–122.

7. Duke L. Kwon and Gregory Thompson, *Reparations: A Christian Call to Repentance and Repair* (Grand Rapids: Brazos, 2021).
8. John Perkins, *With Justice for All: A Strategy for Community Development* (Ventura, CA: Regal, 2007).
9. Kwon and Thompson, *Reparations*, 115–30.
10. Kwon and Thompson, 130.
11. Kwon and Thompson, 138.
12. Kwon and Thompson, 157–69.
13. Martin Luther King Jr., "All Labor Has Dignity," March 18, 1968, in *"All Labor Has Dignity,"* ed. Michael K. Honey (Boston: Beacon, 1986), 171.
14. King, "All Labor Has Dignity," 172–73.

Chapter 1: Jubilee Is Freedom

1. Lowell Noble argues that "the blatant oppression of the more distant past has contributed greatly to the economic disparities of the recent past and the present day. Many white evangelicals try to separate these two phenomena," in *From Oppression to Jubilee Justice* (Jackson, MS: Urban Verses, 2007), 3.
2. That concrete effect is summed up well by Lowell Noble who says that "Jubilee justice is two-pronged: it not only stops oppression and takes measures to prevent the recurrence of injustice, but it also provides access to resources from God's creation so a family can be self-sufficient . . . it releases from oppression, and it provides resources for development." Noble, *From Oppression to Jubilee Justice,* 84.
3. In *The Upside Down Kingdom*, Donald Kraybill calls this "God's social blueprint for his people." Donald Kraybill, *The Upside Down Kingdom* (Scottsdale, PA: Herald Press, 1978), 101, in Noble, *From Oppression to Jubilee Justice,* 86.
4. We are using the term *American* in this context as this is how the term is used colloquially. Obviously, we intend to reflect on the specific values and ideals of the United States, but those values are articulated as "American" and so we chose to mimic the common usage in this regard.
5. Scholars are increasing their attention to the nature of largely

evangelical Christianity's influence on society and complicity in injustice. Examples include Kristin Kobes Du Mez, *Jesus and John Wayne: How White Evangelicals Corrupted a Faith and Fractured a Nation* (2021); Jesse Curtis, *The Myth of Colorblind Christians: Evangelicals and White Supremacy in the Civil Rights Era* (2021); and Randall Balmer, *Bad Faith: Race and the Rise of the Religious Right* (2021), *Evangelicals in America* (2016), *Mine Eyes Have Seen the Glory: A Journey into the Evangelical Subculture in America*, 5th ed. (2014), *First Freedom: The Fight for Religious Liberty* (2012), and *Thy Kingdom Come: How the Religious Right Distorts the Faith and Threatens America* (2006).

6. Howard Thurman, *Jesus and the Disinherited* (Boston: Beacon, 1976), 20.

7. Carl F. H. Henry, *The Uneasy Conscience of Modern Fundamentalism* (Grand Rapids: Eerdmans, 1947), 10.

8. Dietrich Bonhoeffer, *Creation and Fall/Temptation: Two Biblical Studies* (New York: Macmillan, 1959), 37.

9. Allen J. Beck, "Race and Ethnicity of Violent Crime Offenders and Arrestees, 2018," US Department of Justice, January 2021, https://bjs.ojp.gov/content/pub/pdf/revcoa18.pdf, 1.

10. Michael Mascarenhas, "Environmental Inequality and Environmental Justice," in Kenneth Gould and Tammy Lewis, *Twenty Lessons in Environmental Sociology* (New York: Oxford University Press, 2009), 163.

11. Thurman, *Jesus and the Disinherited*, 3.

12. Gustavo Gutierrez, *A Theology of Liberation* (Maryknoll, NY: Orbis, 1973), 36–37.

13. Gutierrez, *A Theology of Liberation*, 36–37.

14. Gutierrez, 36.

15. James Cone, *The Cross and the Lynching Tree* (Maryknoll, NY: Orbis, 2013).

16. For more on Dorothy Day's life and work, see her *Loaves and Fishes: The Inspiring Story of the Catholic Worker Movement* and *The World Will Be Saved by Beauty: An Intimate Portrait of My Grandmother*.

17. Wendell Berry, "Two Economies," in *The Art of the*

Commonplace: The Agrarian Essays of Wendell Berry (Berkley: Counterpoint, 2002), 223.

18. Jennifer Medina, Katie Benner, and Kate Taylor, "Actresses, Business Leaders and Other Wealthy Parents Charged in U.S. College Entry Fraud," *New York Times*, March 12, 2019, https://www.nytimes.com/2019/03/12/us/college-admissions-cheating-scandal.html.

19. Raymond Rivera, *Liberty to the Captives: Our Call to Ministry in a Captive World* (Grand Rapids: Eerdmans, 2012), 2.

20. Maegan Parker Brooks and Davis W. Houck, eds. *The Speeches of Fannie Lou Hamer: To Tell It Like It Is* (Jackson: University Press of Mississippi, 2011), 136.

Chapter 2: Neighborhoods as Ecosystems

1. Willie Jennings, *The Christian Imagination: Theology and the Origins of Race* (New Haven, CT: Yale University Press, 2011), 248.

2. "Not Even Past: Social Vulnerability and the Legacy of Redlining," accessed October 6, 2022, https://dsl.richmond.edu/socialvulnerability/map/#loc=11/40.858/-73.856&city=bronx-ny.

3. Jill Rosen, "Black Students Who Have One Black Teacher Are More Likely to Go to College," HUB, November 12, 2018, https://hub.jhu.edu/2018/11/12/black-students-black-teachers-college-gap/.

4. Valerie Strauss, "Study: Black Students from Poor Families Are More Likely to Graduate from High School If They Have at Least One Black Teacher," *Washington Post*, April 9, 2017, https://www.washingtonpost.com/news/answer-sheet/wp/2017/04/09/study-black-students-from-poor-families-are-more-likely-to-graduate-high-school-if-they-have-at-least-one-black-teacher/.

5. Gustavo Gutierrez, *A Theology of Liberation: Perspectivas: History, Politics, and Salvation* (Maryknoll, NY: Orbis, 1988), 102–3.

6. Martin Luther King Jr., "Letter from a Birmingham Jail," April 16, 1963, https://letterfromjail.com.

7. Cole Arthur Riley, *This Here Flesh: Spirituality, Liberation, and the Stories That Make Us* (New York: Convergent, 2022), 8.

8. Adrienne Maree Brown, *Emergent Strategy: Shaping Change, Changing Worlds* (AK Press, 2017), 42.

9. Frederick Douglass, "If There Is No Struggle, There Is No Progress" (1857), Blackpast, January 25, 2007, https://www .blackpast.org/african-american-history/1857-frederick-douglass -if-there-no-struggle-there-no-progress/.

Interlude: A Healthy Neighborhood

1. Wendell Berry, "Two Economies," in *The Art of Commonplace: The Agrarian Essays of Wendell Berry* (Berkeley: Counterpoint, 2002), 219.

2. Berry, "Two Economies," 223.

3. Berry, 223.

4. Berry, 222.

5. Berry, 234.

6. Berry, 234.

7. Berry, 226–27.

8. Berry, 220.

9. Wendell Berry, "The Idea of a Local Economy," in *The Art of Commonplace: The Agrarian Essays of Wendell Berry* (Berkeley: Counterpoint, 2002), 250.

10. Berry, "Idea of a Local Economy," 259.

11. Berry, 259.

12. "It is the Great Economy, not any little economy, that invests minute particulars with high and final importance. In the Great Economy, each part stands for the whole and is joined to it; the whole is present in the part and is its health." Berry, "Two Economies," 234.

13. Berry, "Idea of a Local Economy," 258.

14. Adam Gustine, *Becoming a Just Church: Cultivating Communities of God's Shalom.* (Downers Grove: InterVarsity Press, 2019); José Humphreys, *Seeing Jesus in East Harlem: What Happens When Churches Show Up and Stay Put* (Downers Grove, IL: InterVarsity Press, 2018).

15. Berry, "Idea of a Local Economy," 260.
16. Berry, "Two Economies," 233, emphasis in the original.
17. Clemens Sedmak, *The Capacity to Be Displaced: Resilience, Mission, and Inner Strength* (Boston: Brill, 2017), 37.
18. Sedmak, "Capacity to Be Displaced," 50.
19. Sedmak, 37.
20. Sedmak, 44.
21. Berry, "Two Economies," 260.
22. Clemans Sedmak, *Enacting Catholic Social Tradition: The Deep Practice of Human Dignity* (Maryknoll, NY: Orbis, 2022), 69–70. Here Sedmak draws on Stefano Zamagni as the originator of this comparison in "The Common Good and the Civil Economy," in *Searching for the Common Good: Philosophical, Theological and Economic Approaches*, ed. Mathias Nebel and Thierry Collaud (Baden-Baden, Germany: Nomos, 2018), 79–98.
23. Sedmak, *Enacting Catholic Social Tradition*, 70.
24. Wendell Berry, *Hannah Coulter* (Washington, DC: Shoemaker and Hoard, 2004), 83.

Chapter 3: Gleaning: Freeing the Edges of Our Fields

1. The US Catholic Bishops, in *Economic Justice for All*, argue that "the prime purpose of this special commitment to the poor is to enable them to become active participants in the life of society. It is to enable *all* persons to share in and contribute to the common good." United States Catholic Bishops, *Economic Justice for All: Pastoral Letter on Catholic Social Teaching and the U.S. Economy*, 1986, https://www.usccb.org/upload/economic_justice_for_all.pdf, 88.
2. "Access to, and use of, the resources of the whole planet constitute the legacy bequeathed to the whole human race." Christopher Wright, *Old Testament Ethics for the People of God* (Downers Grove, IL: InterVarsity Press, 1994), 147.
3. "Chinese Immigration and the Chinese Exclusion Acts," Office of the Historian: U.S. Department of State, accessed October 6, 2022, https://history.state.gov/milestones/1866–1898/chinese-immigration.

4. Benjamin Franklin, "Letter to Peter Collinson" (May 9, 1753), Teaching American History, accessed October 6, 2022, https://teachingamericanhistory.org/document/letter-to-peter-collinson/.

5. "Here's Donald Trump's Presidential Announcement Speech," *Time*, June 16, 2015, https://time.com/3923128/donald-trump-announcement-speech/.

6. Julissa Arce, "Trump's Anti-immigrant Rhetoric Was Never about Legality—It Was about Our Brown Skin," *Time*, August 6, 2019, https://time.com/5645501/trump-anti-immigration-rhetoric-racism/.

7. Arce, "Trump's Anti-immigrant Rhetoric."

8. Tony Hernandez, "A Brief History of Anti-immigrant Propaganda," Immigrant Archive Project, accessed October 6, 2022, https://immigrantarchiveproject.org/brief-history-anti-immigrant-propaganda/.

9. Rosabeth Moss Kanter, "Powerlessness Corrupts," *Harvard Business Review*, July–August 2010, https://hbr.org/2010/07/column-powerlessness-corrupts.

10. Stephen R. Covey, *The 7 Habits of Highly Effective People* (New York: Simon and Schuster, 1989), 219.

11. Wright, *Old Testament Ethics for the People of God*, 149.

12. Other translations suggest Jesus's words convey the notion of life "to the full" (NIV) or, more pointedly, life "to the full, till it overflows" (AMP). This is instructive because Jesus counters the very notion of scarcity by suggesting his purpose is to draw us into relationship with him so that we share in the abundance of God.

13. "In other words, they were to voluntarily limit their profit taking." Timothy Keller, *Generous Justice: How God's Grace Makes Us Just* (New York: Dutton, 2010), 27.

14. "Gleaning (Leviticus 19:9–10)," Theology of Work Project, accessed October 6, 2022, https://www.theologyofwork.org/old-testament/leviticus-and-work/holiness-leviticus-1727/gleaning-leviticus-19910, emphasis in the original.

15. United States Catholic Bishops, *Economic Justice for All*, 24, emphasis in the original.

16. Keller makes this observation as well, saying, "Gleaning was not, however, what would ordinarily be called an act of charity. It enabled the poor to provide for themselves without relying on benevolence" (Keller, *Generous Justice*, 27). Keller also notes the connections between gleaning, Sabbath, and Jubilee, arguing that they are intended to prevent long-term poverty. The insight is important as we also note this triad of ideas frame God's intent for a society that can reset toward an ideal marked by economic flourishing.

17. Louise Zwick, "Alternatives to Economic Libertarianism: Not Just Solidarity, but Fraternity, an Economics of Inclusion," Houston Catholic Worker, July 29, 2017, https://cjd.org /2017/07/29/alternatives-to-economic-libertarianism-not-just -solidarity-but-fraternity-an-economics-of-inclusion/.

18. Christopher Wright makes a similar argument: "Private domin- ion over some of the material resources of the earth does not give a right to consume the entire product of those resources, because dominion always remains trusteeship under God and responsibility for others. There is no necessary or 'sacrosanct' link between what one owns or invests in the productive process and what one can claim as an exclusive right to consume as income in return." Wright, *Old Testament Ethics for the People of God*, 149.

19. Frederick Douglass, "If There Is No Struggle, There Is No Progress" (1857), Blackpast, January 25, 2007, https://www .blackpast.org/african-american-history/1857-frederick-douglass -if-there-no-struggle-there-no-progress/.

20. Wright, *Old Testament Ethics for the People of God*, 174.

Chapter 4: Sabbath: Restoring over Extracting

1. Hannibal B. Johnson, *Black Wall Street: From Riot to Renaissance in Tulsa's Historic Greenwood District* (Fort Worth, TX: Eakin, 1998), 1–6, 27.

2. Johnson, *Black Wall Street*, 9–10, 18.

3. Johnson, 26, 53.

4. Johnson, 5–6.

5. Johnson, 19.

6. Johnson, 20–21.

7. Johnson, 22–23.

8. Johnson, 24.

9. Johnson, 46.

10. Johnson, 35.

11. W. E. B. Du Bois, quoted in Johnson, 51.

12. Johnson, 47.

13. Johnson, 29.

14. Randall Kennedy, in Alfred L. Brophy, *Reconstructing the Dreamland: The Tulsa Riot of 1921* (Oxford: Oxford University Press, 2002), ix.

15. Dan Gordon, "When Deadly Dirt Devastated the Southern Plains," *Denver Post*, May 12, 2011, https://www.denverpost.com/2011/05/12/when-deadly-dirt-devastated-the-southern-plains/.

16. "White flight made racial homogeneity and upward mobility possible in the neighborhoods, schools, and churches of surburbia, so of course the corollary reality for the urban areas left behind was an inverse image of that same homogeneity. Places labeled as the inner city were stigmatized with the social characteristics of poverty and crime in communities populated exclusively by people of color." David Leong, *Race and Place: How Urban Geography Shapes the Journey to Reconciliation* (Downers Grove, IL: InterVarsity Press, 2017), 135. For an excellent treatment of the forces of white flight and the racialized dimensions that drove the development of the suburbs, see Kevin M. Kruse's *White Flight* (Princeton, NJ: Princeton University Press, 2005).

17. Leong, *Race and Place*, 139.

18. There is a lot of gray area here to be sure. We can't draw a straight line between economic injustice and every new coffee shop in an up-and-coming part of town. But, remembering Young, we don't have to name specific offenses to argue that we are collectively responsible for the fruit of inequity born out in society.

19. With reference to Wendell Berry's essay, "People, Land, and Community" in *The Art of Commonplace: The Agrarian Essays of Wendell Berry* (Berkeley: Counterpoint, 2002).

20. Thomas Merton, *Conjectures of a Guilty Bystander* (New York: Doubleday, 1966), 86.

21. Wendell Berry, "The Idea of a Local Economy," in *The Art of Commonplace: The Agrarian Essays of Wendell Berry* (Berkeley: Counterpoint, 2002), 257.

22. Ched Myers, *The Biblical Vision of Sabbath Economics* (Washington, DC: Tell the Word, Church of the Saviour, 2002), 7, emphasis in the original.

23. Maria Harris, *Proclaim Jubilee: A Spirituality for the Twenty-First Century* (Louisville: Westminster John Knox, 1996), 7.

24. Randy Woodley, *Shalom and the Community of Creation: An Indigenous Vision* (Grand Rapids: Eerdmans, 2012), 81.

25. Richard Lowery, *Sabbath and Jubilee* (St. Louis, MO: Chalice, 2000), 2.

26. Woodley, *Shalom and the Community of Creation*, 79.

27. Lowery, *Sabbath and Jubilee*, 86. "In Genesis 1, the world as God intended it is a world of overflowing abundance, shared power, self-restraint, and universal leisure" (63).

28. Norman Wirzba, *Living the Sabbath: Discovering the Rhythms of Rest and Delight* (Grand Rapids: Brazos, 2006), 52.

29. "Rest is *shalom*. God rests at the end of creation because God is able to rest. God's benevolent rule in the universe is unchallenged. Sabbath rest is a celebration of God's enthronement as universal sovereign." Lowery, *Sabbath and Jubilee*, 89. See also Myers engaging Lowery: "It is important to note that this cosmic Sabbath is *not* for the purpose of resting in order to work more. . . . The purpose of this Sabbath is to enjoy the world *forever* . . . abundance as the divine gift, and self-limitation as the appropriate response." Myers, *Biblical Vision of Sabbath Economics*, 10–11.

30. Myers helpfully unpacks the ways in which God is training Israel throughout the Old Testament but specifically in the exodus narrative to understand the notion of enough (Myers, ch. 1).

31. "It functions to disrupt human attempts to 'control' nature and 'maximize the forces of production.'" Myers, 13.

32. "Sabbath, as blessed time, is the cosmic pole around which all other time coheres. Sabbath establishes all of life as a celebration of the worthiness of God and God's created world. Sabbath is a sign of God's benevolent desire for the world. By observing the blessed sabbath, the world expresses gratitude to the God who calls us into flourishing life." Lowery, *Sabbath and Jubilee*, 90.

33. "Sabbath rest is active, not passive. Furthermore, it has meaning only in reference to God's creative work. Sabbath rest is not the absence of work. It is work's fulfillment. It celebrates creative labor. Rather than saying 'no' to work, sabbath says 'enough for now.'" Lowery, 93.

34. "As individual alienation increases and a sense of social solidarity declines, as the boundaries of time and place that once defined the world of work disappear into cyberspace, sabbath speaks a word of proportion, limits, social solidarity, and the need for rest, quiet reflection, and nonconsumptive recreation. In the emerging world, sabbath consciousness may be the key to human survival, prosperity, and sanity." Lowery, 4.

35. Wirzba, *Living the Sabbath*, 120.

36. "Along the lines of Christian Sunday as a 'little Easter,' biblical sabbath is a 'little sabbath year,' a 'little jubilee.' It is an enduring sign in Israel of the social solidarity and economic justice implied in seventh-year debt release." Lowery, *Sabbath and Jubilee*, 5.

37. Lowery, 62.

38. "Sabbath regulations represent God's strategy for teaching Israel about its dependence upon the land as a gift to share equitably, not as a possession to exploit." Myers, *Biblical Vision of Sabbath Economics*, 13.

39. Some may point to the difference noted in debt forgiveness to family and neighbors and the exclusion of the foreigner from this command. Lowery argues that this is likely because more local loans were "subsistence loans" that helped people get through economically vulnerable situations. The loans to foreigners were related to international trade and thus were

not as likely to be emergency or subsistence loans. Further, resident aliens were well protected in the economic laws of the Old Testament, so foreigners living locally would have been included in the protections envisioned by God and never excluded. "The resident alien is part of the network of mutual support between village households. So subsistence loans to resident aliens are more likely included among the loans to 'your neighbor, your kin.' . . . The issue is not the ethnicity of the borrower, but the nature of the loan. Subsistence help for (foreign) travelers was offered as a gift, not a loan—an act of hospitality, not a debt to be repaid. Loans to 'foreigners'— this is, nonresidents who fall outside the network of clan support—are by their very nature trade loans." Lowery, *Sabbath and Jubilee*, 40.

40. Myers, *Biblical Vision of Sabbath Economics*, 14–15.
41. Myers, 12ff.
42. Lowery, *Sabbath and Jubilee*, 32.
43. "The deuteronomists believe that the creditor who receives the maximum term of service has been more than sufficiently compensated for the original loan. Sharing the surplus is only fair." Lowery, 32.
44. "Proper sabbath observance requires active concern for the welfare of the poor." Lowery, 146.
45. Lowery, 106.
46. "Fires—at least the ones that required kindling—were lighted in or just outside the home for cooking. The fire ban ensures that Israelite householders will not expect the women to "fire up the oven" and cook, while the men enjoy sabbath-day rest. Sabbath knows no distinction of gender . . . the sabbath ban of lighting fires addresses the same concern that lies in the background of the sabbath-manna story. . . . No one will be forced to work on the sabbath. Male or female, slave or free— everyone is freed from toil." Lowery, 108.
47. Lowery, 109.
48. Lowery, 121.
49. "Sabbath was never entirely ceremonial. . . . Sabbath included the regular practice of justice." Harris, *Proclaim Jubilee*, 31.

50. Myers, *Biblical Vision of Sabbath Economics*.
51. Myers, 14.
52. Lowery, *Sabbath and Jubilee*.
53. "The basic sabbath narratives celebrate a world of abundance, self-restraint, and social solidarity . . . a world of lavish abundance where everyone works who is able, everyone rests when her or his body requires rest, and every household has what it needs to survive." Lowery, 146.

Chapter 5: Jubilee: Justice That Circles Back

1. "Bills about Armed Forces and National Security Sponsored by Raphael Warnock (D-Ga.)," ProPublica, accessed November 21, 2022, https://projects.propublica.org/represent /members/W000790/bills-for-category/armed-forces-and -national-security/117.
2. Julia C. Mead, "Memories of Segregation in Levittown," *New York Times*, May 11, 2003. https://www.nytimes.com /2003/05/11/nyregion/memories-of-segregation-in-levittown .html.
3. Frederick Douglass, "If There Is No Struggle, There Is No Progress" (1857), Blackpast, January 25, 2007, https://www .blackpast.org/african-american-history/1857-frederick-douglass -if-there-no-struggle-there-no-progress/.
4. N. Sherwin-White, quoted in Obery Hendricks, *The Politics of Jesus: Rediscovering the True Revolutionary Nature of Jesus' Teachings and How They Have Been Corrupted* (New York: Three Leaves, 2007), 61.
5. Walter Brueggemann, *A Gospel of Hope* (Louisville: Westminster John Knox, 2018), 73.
6. "Eco-Theology and Zoning Meetings: An Interview with Willie Jennings," Reflections, accessed October 7, 2022, https:// reflections.yale.edu/article/crucified-creation-green-faith-rising /eco-theology-and-zoning-meetings-interview-willie.
7. "Eco-Theology and Zoning Meetings."
8. On the Commons, accessed November 21, 2022, http://www .onthecommons.org/about-commons#sthash.lsG5BAtL.dpbs.
9. Mark Charles and Soong-Chan Rah, *Unsettling Truths: The*

Ongoing, Dehumanizing Legacy of the Doctrine of Discovery (Downers Grove, IL: InterVarsity Press, 2019), 194.

10. George Tinker, quoted in Emily McFarlan Miller, "Churches Return Land to Indigenous Groups as Part of #LandBack Movement," November 26, 2020, https://religionnews.com /2020/11/26/churches-return-land-to-indigenous-groups-amid -repentance-for-role-in-taking-it-landback-movement/.

11. Miller, "Churches Return Land to Indigenous Groups."

12. "Racial and Gender Disparities in the Sex Trade," Rights4Girls, accessed November 21, 2022, https://rights4girls .org/wp-content/uploads/2019/05/Racial-Disparties-FactSheet -_Jan-2021.pdf.

13. "5 Companies Radically Shaped by the Faith of Their Owners," CT Creative Studio, April 20, 2020, https://www.christianity today.com/partners/c12/5-companies-radically-shaped-by-faith -of-their-owners.html.

14. Rebecca Maxon, "Stress in the Workplace: A Costly Epidemic," *FDU Magazine*, Summer 1999, https://portal.fdu.edu/newspubs /magazine/99su/stress.html.

Interlude: The Jubilee of Jesus: Our Manifesto

1. Shane Claiborne and Chris Haw unpack this idea in *Jesus for President: Politics for Ordinary Radicals* (Grand Rapids: Zondervan, 2008).

2. Claiborne and Haw, *Jesus for President*, 88.

3. Tim Soerens, *Everywhere You Look: Discovering the Church Right Where You Are* (Downers Grove, IL: InterVarsity Press, 2020), 69.

4. Ron Sider, *Rich Christians in an Age of Hunger: Moving from Affluence to Generosity*, 6th ed. (Nashville: Thomas Nelson, 2015), 43–44.

5. Alexia Salvatierra and Brandon Wrencher, *Buried Seeds: Learning from the Vibrant Resilience of Marginalized Christian Communities* (Grand Rapids: Baker Academic, 2022), 60.

6. Lynne Twist, *The Soul of Money: Transforming Your*

Relationship with Money and Life (New York: Norton, 2017), 51.

Chapter 6: Gleaning: An Economy of Sharing and Opportunity

1. Willie James Jennings, *Acts* (Louisville: Westminster John Knox, 2017), 50.
2. We note that the term *sharing economy* is in popular use to describe systems that allow for individuals to share specific resources and assets. This is certainly in mind as we write. Our hope is to expand that sense of sharing to ways of creating economic opportunity for the poor and vulnerable.
3. "5. Mutual Benefit," National Humanities Center," accessed October 7, 2022, http://nationalhumanitiescenter.org/pds /maai/community/text5/text5read.htm.
4. Roxie Hammill, "Millions in Crushing Medical Debt—Gone. All Thanks to These Churches," *USA Today*, May 31, 2019, https://www.usatoday.com/story/news/2019/05/31/church-pays -medical-bills-debt-rip-medical-debt/1286600001/.
5. Ada Maria Isasi-Diaz, *Mujerista Theology: A Theology for the Twenty-First Century* (Maryknoll, NY: Orbis, 1996).

Chapter 7: Sabbath: An Economy of Restoration

1. Majora Carter, *Reclaiming Your Community: You Don't Have to Move Out of Your Neighborhood to Live in a Better One* (Oakland, CA: Berrett-Koehler, 2022), 23.
2. Carter, *Reclaiming Your Community*, 25.
3. James Rebanks, *English Pastoral: An Inheritance* (Westminster: Allen Lane, 2020), 102.
4. Learn more at risestjames.org.

Chapter 8: Jubilee: An Economy of Ownership and Celebration

1. Eric Foner, *Reconstruction: America's Unfinished Revolution 1863–1877*, repr. ed. (Savannah, GA: History Book Club, 2005), 71.

2. Foner, *Reconstruction*, 71.

3. Foner, 71.

4. Foner, 70.

5. Perry Yoder says these laws (Sabbath and Jubilee) "tackled the matter of access . . . These laws were a type of economic reform legislation to redistribute the capital resources of the community so that they would not become concentrated in the hands of a few." Perry Yoder, *Shalom* (Newton, KS: Faith and Life Press, 1987), 81, in Noble, 86.

6. Transform Capital, accessed November 21, 2022, https:// tccommunity.org/.

7. A. A. Cristi, "The Cultural Space Agency's and Cultivate South Park Announce 'El Barrio' Acquisition," Broadway World, May 2, 2022, https://www.broadwayworld.com/denver/article /The-Cultural-Space-Agencys-And-Cultivate-South-Park -Announce-El-Barrio-Acquisition-20220502.

Postlude: Beyond the Two Americas

1. Norman Wirzba, *Living the Sabbath: Discovering the Rhythms of Rest and Delight* (Grand Rapids: Brazos, 2006), 117.

2. Christine Firer Hinze, *Radical Sufficiency: Work, Livelihood, and a US Catholic Economic Ethic* (Georgetown: Georgetown University Press, 2021), 250. Firer Hinze's work is exemplary, for our purposes the insights drawn in the final two chapters are a compelling vision for the work of solidarity toward economic justice and life in community.

3. Firer Hinze, *Radical Sufficiency*, 273.

4. Martin Luther King Jr., "Remaining Awake through a Great Revolution," Oberlin College commencement address, June 1965, https://www2.oberlin.edu/external/EOG/Black HistoryMonth/MLK/CommAddress.html.

5. Firer Hinze, *Radical Sufficiency*, 271. "For *Homo solidarietus*, market economy and market competition are always embedded in and answerable to cooperative and reciprocal relationships and communities."

6. Rebecca Todd Peters, "Considering a Solidarity Economy as a Framework for Justice" in *The Almighty and the Dollar:*

Reflections on Economic Justice for All, ed. Mark J. Allman (Winona, MN: Anselm Academic, 2012), 132.
7. Firer Hinze, *Radical Sufficiency*, 271.
8. Firer Hinze, 272.
9. Firer Hinze, 271.